Know Your Zombies

Ed Wenck and Lou Harry

BLUE RIVER PRESS

Blue River Press
Indianapolis, Indiana

Cover Design: Phil Velikan
Cover Illustration Provided by: Dave Aikins
Layout: MaryKay Hruskocy Scott
Interior Illustrations Provided by: Paris Chrisopoulos
Proofread by: MaryKay Hruskocy Scott

Printed in the United States of America
10 9 8 7 6 5 4 3 2 1

Blue River Press
Distributed by Cardinal Publishers Group
Tom Doherty Company, Inc.
www.cardinalpub.com

Ed: For every late-night creature-feature pre-cable-TV emcee, from the Ghost Host in Baltimore to Sammy Terry in Indianapolis.

Lou: For the good folks at the long-gone Sharpe's newsstand in Wildwood, New Jersey, who sold me my first issue of *Famous Monsters of Filmland* magazine.

Table of Contents

Introduction: Zombies and Why We Love Them

It's hard to believe, in a pop culture world populated with *The Walking Dead*, *Pride and Prejudice with Zombies*, and *Shaun of the Dead*, that zombies were once the unwanted stepchildren of horror films.

It doesn't take a visit to your Netflix queue to see that the silent movie horror era was dominated by the personality packed creations of Lon Chaney, Jr. (*The Phantom of the Opera*, *The Hunchback of Notre Dame*, et. al) and that the black-and-white classics of the '30s and '40s usually had the names Frankenstein or Dracula attached. And in the '50s and '60s, British horror film company Hammer took over with Frankenstein monsters and vampires of their own.

These charismatic creations and others of their ilk (the Wolfman, the Mummy, etc.), whether played by Boris Karloff, Bela Lugosi, Lon Chaney, Jr. or Christopher Lee, had one thing in common: They were individuals. Yes, they may be out for blood, but they weren't anonymous. Each had a distinct personality. And when they finally were vanquished, there wasn't an army of them ready to take their place.

And they had names.

It's interesting that, for most of cinematic history, filmmakers gave names to their nightmares. And, in a sense, by naming them they exercised a degree of control over these creatures. Naming and taming are very similar. When we give something a name, we give it parameters. Limits.

Then there are zombies.

Sure, zombies existed in entertainment before George Romero gave us *Night of the Living Dead*, but they were largely under the monster movie radar. What that Pittsburgh-based auteur did was see the chill value in their facelessness. Think about it: It's one thing to fear the limited number of zombies being created by Bela Lugosi in *White Zombie*. It's another to combat one flesh-hungry zombie knowing that there are hundreds of others that have his back—and are willing to step over it to get to you.

Such relentlessness is a core element in the zombies we've seen since Romero's midnight movie classic. And that tidal wave of terror vibe keeps us tuning in.

How to Use This Book

Know Your Zombies is a combination guide book/puzzle book/ trivia book. We hope it helps bring back great memories of your favorite zombie movies, introduce you to some you may have missed, and challenge your knowledge of your favorite horror movie genre.

Which quizzes and puzzles are right for you?

Of course, you can try them all. But we've also rated them for degree of difficulty.

As a rule of sliced-off-thumb, if you can't name more than three of the George Romero zombie films, don't know who Tor Johnson was, and/or can't remember whether *28 Days* is the zombie film or the movie where Sandra Bullock goes to rehab, then you should probably stick with the DefCon 1-labeled challenges.

If, on the other hand, you can quote dialogue from any zombie flick, have shaken hands with Tom Savini, have seen the musical *Zombie Prom* (without having been in it) and/or have feasted on the flesh of the living, then you probably should jump up to DefCon 3 puzzlers.

If you are somewhere in between, then you are on your own in DefCon 2.

In addition to its use as a fun, pencil-pushing read, *Know Your Zombies* can also be used as:

1. A not-very effective weapon. Throwing this book at an approaching zombie isn't likely to buy more than a second of extra time for you on this earth.
2. A time-killer while you wait in your bunker for the zombies to starve or move along.
3. Kindling, should the fire in your camp die out just when you hear disturbing, hungry sounds out there in the darkness.

Zombies 101: What They Are and How to Get Away

While Hollywood has certainly popularized zombies, the walking dead have been a part of popular culture since long before the advent of cinema. The dead get up and walk in as wide-ranging sources as The Bible and *La Morte de Arthur* (one of the original King Arthur tellings).

But, of course, Lazurus and the guy brought back by Lancelot du Lac didn't let a hunger for human flesh get the better of them. For that, you'll have to turn to *The Epic of Gilgamesh*, which includes a reference to Ishtar summoning the dead to "eat the living."

Actually, zombies are rooted in Haitian culture, where the word "zombie" translates as "spirit of the dead."

One of many academic courses about zombies that have sprung up in the last decade was recently taught at the University of Baltimore. Professor Arnold Blumberg, who's conducted an-all-zombie-semester class in media genres (part of UB's pop-culture minor) feels that zombies change from decade to decade to give us a mirror on where we are as Americans—especially with regards to race and 'the others'; those who are foreign both in looks and spirituality.

"The zombie has become an umbrella term for a wide range of creatures that reflect where we are as a culture," says Blumberg, pointing out that the early critters depicted in *White Zombie* and *I Walked with a Zombie* were a misinformed take on the voodoo myths that came out of the West Indies.

According to Blumberg, in Haitian voodoo a zombie was a living, breathing person who roamed about in a somnambulistic state brought on by drugs, incantations or a handy combination platter of the two. The zombie was controlled by a high priest—and the zombie was commanded to do their bidding.

Haitian voodoo practice called for the introduction of *coup padre*, a substance made from the poisonous porcupine fish, to be ingested by the subject who was to be zombiefied. The heart rate slowed and motor functions dissipated to their point where the ghoul-to-be appeared dead enough to warrant burial by his family and friends. Surviving that, he or she—now devoid of memory—would be exhumed by a high priest or 'Bokor', who'd have dominion over the poor sap until the priest himself expired. (Not a big leap from 'zombie' to 'slave', eh?)

Early zombie flicks were about racial fears and a suspicion of the exotic Caribbean culture that yielded strange religious rituals and really spicy foods. Blumberg says that since there wasn't a big cache of European folklore to draw from (as there was for vampires and wolf-people) the great B-movie maestros were pretty much free to make it up as they went along. The interpretation of the 'zombie' from lumbering irradiated flesh-eater to infected victim to video-game-points-target matches up nearly decade by decade as a symbol of what really scares—and entertains us—here in the Western world.

Zombies 201: When Is a Zombie Not a Zombie?

Okay, okay, stop yelling.

We're certain there are purists aplenty thumbing through this tome raging that the rage virus from *28 Days Later* doesn't kill you, it just makes you angry, that *Planet Terror*'s ghouls were merely gassed-up living beings and *[REC]*, well . . . okay. We get it. Danny Boyle and Alex Garland, director and writer of *28 Days Later*, respectively, even went out of their way to point out that their crazed critters were very much alive—just amped-up on very, very bad bacteria.

Some zombies are non-zombies—heck, even Haitian Voodoo zombies aren't George Romero zombies, they're just folks who've been drugged to *look* dead. If you're peeved that some very-nearly-okay-almost-not-quite zombie flicks have made our list of movies, we could argue that given the original definition and explanation of 'zombie' as a living thing, *Night of the Living Dead* isn't really a zombie flick. Conversely, we could argue that the whole *Frankenstein* canon deserves to be here. (Why should we hold it against him that the Doc's monster is made from multiple corpses?)

Yep—we could spend weeks quibbling about the inclusion of some movies in this book and the exclusion of some others; but doesn't that just devour the fun right of the midsection of what we're trying to do here?

For more also-rans (or, is it, also shuffles?), see Near Zombies on page 148.

White Zombie (1932)

In the beginning there was . . . *White Zombie*.

While the film has its predecessors, *White Zombie* is widely considered the first film in the genre.

Set in a superstition-laden version of Haiti, the film concerns a couple who quickly find that their visit to the island isn't the ideal site for their wedding. In fact, their host, in love with his female guest, hires a guy with the wonderful name of Murder Legendre (Bela Lugosi, of course) to turn her into a zombie.

This being an early example of the genre, you won't find brain-eating or limb removal in *White Zombie*'s zombies. Instead, Legandre uses one of those patented Hollywood secret potions—one of those that drains the life from its victims. Bela and his shuffling pals then steal her body and bring her back to, well, not exactly life.

Which, of course, disappoints Legandre's customer, who was hoping for the gal he fell for and not a member of the vacant-eyed undead. Rather than try to make his customer happy, Legandre gives him a dose of the poison. Thank goodness for him there wasn't a Better Business Bureau to report him to.

After that, things really get messy in this barely-over-an-hour flick, with a local missionary squaring off with the zombie army and the conflicted woman resisting an order from Legendre to knock off her husband.

End result: Legendre and our host do battle and fall to their deaths, the zombies—out of Legenre's control—take lemming-like dives (Okay, purists, actual lemmings don't really do that, but you know what we're talking about), and, surprise, our heroine never really died, she only was very, very sleepy or something, thus allowing the couple to live happily ever after. With a few nightmares, of course.

While the film is held up as one of Lugosi's better works (that's not saying too much), *White Zombie* isn't held with nearly the regard that Frankenstein, The Wolf Man, and Dracula are. Yet the film proved a big box office hit. But the problem with zombies—unlike, say Frankenstein's monster or Dracula—is that the creatures are largely interchangeable. So the prospect of a sequel didn't seem to be on anyone's mind.

Lugosi did go on to make a handful of other zombie films, including *Bowery at Midnight* (1942), *Voodoo Man* (1944), and *Zombies on Broadway* (1945). None had the impact of his first.

White Zombie Quiz
Answers on page 162.

Rating: DefCon 1

1. True of False: Actress Madge Bellemy, who plays Madeleine, was later arrested for shooting her wealthy boyfriend.

2. True or False: *White Zombie* began as a stage play.

3. At the time of the release of *White Zombie*, was the U.S. still occupying Haiti?

4. Who is the first character to say the word "zombies"?

Rating: DefCon 2

5. What does Legendre carve with his knife on the couple's wedding night?

6. What color suit is the groom wearing?

7. What instrument does the zombiefied bride play?

8. The corpses in *White Zombie* were, in part, created by the same legendary make-up man who crafted the iconic Frankenstein monster look for Boris Karloff. Take a stab at naming that make-up man.

9. Complete one of the movie's tag lines: "What does a man want in a woman, is it her _____ or her _____?"

10. What newspaper's critic said: "All the actors have strange lines to say, but appear to enjoy saying them."

I Walked with a Zombie (1942)

For all the undead that shuffled through the movies of the 1930s and '40s, cinema still didn't have a zombie classic.

Enter Val Lewton who took over the RKO Studios horror department with a self-imposed mandate of creating the kind of suspense films that he himself liked. That meant less attention to make-up-covered monsters or overt violence and a greater emphasis on creepiness and cinematic poetry.

The first of these was, well, that's a trivia question for the end of the section. The second of these was *I Walked with a Zombie* (1943), directed by Jacques Tourneur.

Plot isn't as important as atmosphere in Lewton-produced films, but here's how it goes. A nurse comes to the island of San Sebastian to care for a plantation owner's wife—a woman who has reportedly been turned into . . . yep, that's right. Complicating matters is the nurse falling for the plantation owner and the rumor that his wife may have had an affair with the owner's half-brother who is now interested in the nurse and, well, this is sounding more like *General Hospital* than a zombie film.

Willing to make a leap beyond traditional medicine (which doesn't seem to be working), the nurse escorts her charge to the local voodoo church in search of a cure. There, she encounters the bug-eyed, shirtless native zombie Carrefour, who became the poster boy for zombies for decades—at least, until George Romero and company came along.

Later, the voodoo-practicing folks sic Carrefour on the nurse, crazed step-brother kills his half-sister-in-law, and a lot of questions are left unanswered. But that feels less to do with sloppy screenwriting than with a deliberate effort by Lewton and Tourneur to create an atmosphere of uncertainty.

In this world of shadows, nobody has all the answers.

I Walked with a Zombie (1942) Quiz
Answers on page 162.

Rating: DefCon 1
1. Val Lewton also produced a classic feline horror film. Name it.

2. The title was taken from a:
   a. comic book
   b. magazine article
   c. memoir
   d. campaign slogan

Rating: DefCon 2
3. What is the first line of the movie?

4. Curt Siodmak wrote the original script for *I Walked with a Zombie*. What classic horror film monster did he help created?

5. Where are the heroine and the zombie walking when the film opens?

Rating: DefCon 3
6. How was the traditional disclaimer before *I Walked with a Zombie* altered?

7. The same year as *I Walked with a Zombie*, Manton Moreland and John Carradine starred in a sequel/remake of 1941's comedy *King of the Zombies*. Name it.

Acroustic

Rating: DefCon 2

New to acrostics? Here's how they work. Answer whatever questions you can from the clues on the next page. Next, transfer the letters from your answers to the appropriate spots on the grid. By working back and forth, you're goal is to come up with a quote from the classic zombie film *Dawn of the Dead*. We've provided a few starter letters for you. Solution on page 169.

1	2	3	4 R	5		6	7	8	9		10	11	12	13		14	15	16	17
	18 I	19		20	21	22		23	24	25	26	27	28	29	30	31	32	33	34
	35	36	37	38	39	40	41		42	43	44		45	46		47	48	49	50
.		51 I	52		53	54	55	56		57	58 P		59	60	61		62 K	63	64
65	66 !	82		67	68	69		70	71	72	73	74	75		76	77		78	79
80	81	82		83	84	85		86	87		88	89	90		91	92	93	94 !	

1. ___ ___ ___ ___ ___ ___ ___
   47 23 27 39 18 67 1
   Burrowing insect.

2. ___ ___ ___ ___
   93 76 65 38
   Stitch's Disney partner.

3. ___ ___ ___ ___
   50 21 8 89
   Sound zombies make.

4. ___ ___ ___ ___ ___
   20 92 83 68 52
   _____ of the Living Dead.

5. ___ ___ ___ ___ ___ ___ ___ ___
   36 13 3 22 33 69 14 48
   Dental foursome.

6. __ __ __ __ __ __ __
56 40 2 84 30 77 15

Numeric rank of dangerous Biblical seal.

7. __ __ __ __ __ __
82 44 24 55 26 17

More than a quintet.

8. __ __ __ __ __
6 72 90 53 75

Avoid, or a make of car useful in avoiding zombies.

9. __ __ __ __ __ __ __ __ __
9 49 66 37 71 60 12 7 34

Gone deeper.

10. __ __ __ __ __ __ __ __ __
94 11 80 74 5 87 45 70 41

Kid candy on a stick.

11. __ __ __ __ __ __ __ __
61 88 85 31 35 59 43 91

Collection of information.

12. __ __ __ __ __ __
28 16 78 54 86 73

Tom Savini did this for *Day of the Dead*.

13. __ __ __ __
25 42 46 57

The soy in your miso.

14. __ __
79 32

Roddy McDowell film about a Golem.

15. __ __ __ __ __
10 63 64 89 19

Things you don't enjoy paying.

Solution on page 170.

Across

1. Type of year that killers "The Night Stalker" Ramirez and "Monster" Wuornos were born
5. *Apprentice* host who played himself in *Ghosts Can't Do It*
10. With 9-Down, name of noted make-up artist for 40-Across
14. Estimator's words (2 wds.)
15. Jane nickname for *Barbarella* star
16. Burn remedy from a plant
17. Dominant Mr. Sardonicus feature
18. Place where creature is found in *Frankenstein Meets the Wolf Man* (2 wds.)
19. Safecracker
20. World-weary
22. Separate wheat from chaff
24. Had a fried-brain sandwich
25. Masked strike caller
28. Big heart?
29. Crew equipment used as a weapon in "Dead Island" game
32. Bell and Barker
33. Palindromic half-wit
35. Continue to exist, as a vampire
37. Beat, and how!
39. Acts as the interlocutor
40. Film featuring the work of 9- and 48-Down (2 wds.)
43. Diva's solo in *Evenings in Quarantine: The Zombie Opera*
45. *Three's Company* couple
46. Soup bean
49. Agile, like Spider-Man
50. The Fly's chemical enemy
53. Put two and two together
54. Heart of the matter
56. Thumbs-up vote
57. Eternally, in poems
58. Work the crowd at Monstermania

61. "Keep that out of this neighborhood" acronym
63. Slasher movie: ___ to Rest (2009)
65. Moved like the Blob
68. IMDb life stories, for short
69. Look like a wolf
70. "Pardon me!"
71. Ain't right?
72. With 48-Down, star of 40-Across
73. Mirror phenomenon
74. Gets the picture

Down

1. Immovable pileup
2. Typos in *The Zombie Survival Guide*
3. Comments to the audience
4. Corn cake
5. However, briefly
6. Sprinted away from a zombie
7. The U in ICU
8. Coffee shop order
9. See 10-Across
10. Blue birds
11. Mr. Hyde's tavern
12. Gear tooth
13. 15.5-gallon barrel of White Zombie Ale
21. Persian Gulf emirate
23. When vampires begin to come out, in verse
26. Shed one's skin
27. Gondolier, e.g.
30. Word in title of first Indiana Jones film
31. Hi-___ graphics
34. TV clowns
36. Speaker's platform
37. One of the Five Ws.
38. Plant that put the Cowardly Lion to sleep

40. Climactic location in *Frankenstein* (1931)
41. Like mortals?
42. *X-Men* director, ___ Singer
43. St. with a red X on its flag
44. Kevin Smith horror flick, ___ *State*
47. Early Hitchcock thriller, *Jamaica* ___
48. See 72-Across
50. Untimely end for a movie monster
51. Remove the skeleton from a corpse
52. Lovers' secret meetings
55. Star of 1963's *The Haunting*, Claire ___
59. Creative spark for a movie plot
60. Actor and special effects tech for *Teenage Zombie House Massacre*, ___ Haidet
62. Bird venerated by ancient Egyptians
63. Soft toss
64. Obituary datum
66. Work unit
67. Turn red, perhaps

Sudokill

Rating: DefCon 2

Sudoku puzzles have taken over the world faster than faster than the running ghouls in the remake of *Dawn of the Dead*. Nonetheless, there's still a chance that you've never tried one—or never tried one that uses body parts instead of numbers. Your goal is to fill in the blanks so that each body part only appears once in each row, once in each column, and once in each 3 x 3 square (indicated by bolded lines). Solution on page 169.

SCALP			FOOT			RIB		
TOE			EYEBALL			BRAIN		
NOSE			EAR			TOOTH		

TOE	EAR		SCALP			EYE BALL		
FOOT		EYE BALL		TOE				NOSE
			NOSE					
EYE BALL	TOE						TOOTH	FOOT
		BRAIN			FOOT		SCALP	RIB
			BRAIN	RIB				EYE BALL
	FOOT				TOE			TOE
			TOE	NOSE	TOOTH	EAR		
TOOTH	BRAIN						NOSE	

Teenage Zombies (1959)

If Ed Wood was the single worst filmmaker to ever pick up a camera, he had some pretty serious competition from the helmsman of *Teenage Zombies*. Jerry Warren already had laughers like *Man Beast* and *The Incredible Petrified World* under his belt before he shot this grade-Z cult epic that featured roughly 20 minutes of plot and more footage of people walking than a treadmill infomercial.

Even though Warren's actors were only slightly more animated than your average cord of firewood and Warren himself had zero sense of pacing, lighting, camera placement or shot composition, *Teenage Zombies* is weirdly compelling. There are elements of this black-and-white block of cheese that actually work; notably, the storyline itself. Four kids go off to water-ski, wind up on a remote island, and are imprisoned by an evil female scientist, Dr. Myra (Katherine Victor, who has a thing for arm bracelets. Sexy.). The kids are locked up—clearly an excuse to put two nubile blonde gals together in a cage—while Dr. Myra is visited by a pair of agents who seem to have some connection to the Soviet bloc.

Dr. Myra has been working on a formula that enslaves her subjects— her primary zombie-fied henchman is a lumbering gent who looks like a cross between Frankenstein's monster and an Old Spice TV commercial sailor after a serious bender. The agents warn that if Myra doesn't pick up the pace, their Rooskie bosses will level the States with H-bombs. Back on the mainland, two kids who chose horseback riding over skiing realize their pals are loooong overdue and enlist the local sheriff (Mike Concannon) to help search for the missing teens.

Alas, the sheriff is in on Dr. Kyra's evildoings—he's been providing drunks and prisoners to the doc for her nefarious experiments. The constable is more than a little peeved that Myra is about to use law-abiding kids as her next subjects, and commie agent Whorf (Steve Conte) guns him down. Fortunately for the youngsters, male prisoners Reg (Don Sullivan) and Skip (Paul Pepper) have gotten loose. Myra gasses the two blondes before Reg and Skip can free them from their room full of toxic fumes, and the girls become mindless minions of Myra. The Worst Fight Scene Ever Shot ensues—which is ultimately settled by an enslaved gorilla (yes, a gorilla) who is released from his mental captivity by the same antidote that cures the girls.

The picture is loaded with gaps in logic, for example: super secret island lairs for wannabe Communist world-conquerors have really cheap locks and zero security measures. As woefully hysterical as the script is, there are one or two ideas in the mix that turned up in later zombie flicks: the gas works differently on each individual, and some *rage* (I'm lookin' at you, Danny Boyle), while others are simply hypnotized.

The 'zombies' here don't die, they're merely doped-up servants of a master of a manner that clearly links the film to its roots in Haitian mythology. Additionally, the notion that the world is on the verge of apocalypse—zombie or nuclear, depending on the Kremlim's whims—pre-dated Romero's visions by a decade.

While a great many members of the cast who appeared in *Teenage Zombies* never turned up in films again, the movie did mark a point in the arc of one or two fascinating careers. Katherine Victor clearly learned what not to do during her tenure as one of Jerry Warren's regulars and went on to handle continuity co-ordination for dozens upon dozens of Disney's animated television shows and movies. She modeled and handled real estate, and always felt that her association with Warren's lousy productions hamstrung her acting career.

Brianne Murphy, who played blonde cutie Pam, had been a rodeo trick rider and circus clown before she wound up working for—and briefly becoming the spouse of—Jerry Warren. She went on to shoot and direct numerous projects, becoming the first ever female director of a unionized, major-studio production, the Dom Deluise vehicle *Fatso* (1980). As for Warren, the man behind the madness went on to produce campy classics such as *The Wild World of Batwoman* (featured on *Mystery Science Theatre 3000*) and *Frankenstein Island*—starring John Carradine.

Teenage Zombies, though, remains the low-water mark for Warren, even though lines about politicians meddling in science seem oddly prescient today. The laughable production quality—complete with washout lighting and a guy in a bad monkey-suit—plus the fact that nearly all of the score was lifted *without credit* from the 1957 flick *Kronos* cemented Warren's rep as a true auteur of awful.

Teenage Zombies Quiz
Answers on page 162.

Answers on page 162.

Rating: DefCon 1
1. Which of the following is not the name of a '50s horror film:
    a. *I was a Teenage Frankenstein*
    b. *I was a Teenage Werewolf*
    c. *Teen Dracula*
    d. *Teenage Cave Man*

Rating: DefCon 2
2. What is the name of Dr. Myra's lumbering henchman?

Rating: DefCon 3
3. What is Campus House?

The Plague of the Zombies (1966)

Shot two years prior and an ocean away from *Night of the Living Dead*, *The Plague of the Zombies* is also stylistically light years distant from Romero's game-changer. *Plague* had the look and feel of everything coming out of Britain's Hammer studios in the '50s and '60s—it seems much more like a vampire film than the modern zombie epics we're treated to nowadays. It's mannered, it's Victorian, it's oh-so-very-*very*-British. Shot back-to-back on the same sets in lavish grindhouse fashion with *The Reptile*, *Plague* was intended for release as the lesser half of a double bill that included *Dracula: Prince of Darkness*. The latter starred one of Hammer's biggest box-office draws, the iconic Christopher Lee, but the studio's only foray into zombie-dom still managed to become a beloved entry in its own genre.

Set in Cornwall, England, in 1860, *The Plague of the Zombies* opens with a voodoo ritual, complete with jungle drums and some really terrible African stereotypes. A gent in a creepy death-mask dribbles blood on a small doll—a woman sleeping elsewhere reacts violently—and before you know it, the local doctor is sending out for reinforcements. Seems the townsfolk in Cornwall are keeling over at the rate of one per month, and young Doc Peter Thompson (Brook Williams) calls for his mentor, Sir James Forbes (Andre Morell), who beats a path to the countryside with lithesome daughter Sylvia (Diane Clare) along to say hi to her old pal, Mrs. Alice Thompson (Jacqueline Pearce).

A creeping malaise is gripping the village! A dead man's brother has spotted the corpse of his sibling strolling about! Alice becomes ill—and succumbs! Sylvia is threatened by 'The Youngbloods', a gang of lads who live with the local squire, a gent named Hamilton (John Carson), who looks a little like Peter Cushing and sounds a lot like James Mason. After a few very wry strokes of his mustache, it doesn't take long for the wise, Sherlock-Holmes-like Forbes to figure out that the village squire is engaging in rituals to enslave the undead to work in his tin mine. (The townsfolks believes that mine's haunted, y'see, guv-ner, and the squire's had trouble gettin'a single bloke to work down there . . .)

As with a great many Hammer films, the flick is long on exposition and mood-building and keeps the bloody bits to a minimum—but *Plague* is critical because it develops some of the zombie movies' best known tenets. First—and this may be the first time ever in any film it's seen on screen—beheading a zombie, even if she's your best pupil's dead wife, is a really effective way to deal with the undead. Secondly, the zombie 'look' we've grown accustomed too—the gray pallor, odd and vacant eyes, might-be-rotting-flesh/might-be-old-Play-Doh makeup—it's all here, slowly lumbering toward the living . . . not to eat. Just to do the master's bidding. And perhaps most importantly, Doctor Thompson's nightmare in which zombies attack from all sides must have been known to George Romero—it's a shot he and many, many others have imitated countless times.

Hammer Films had first ventured into the horror genre in 1955, and leaned heavily on its major stars, Cushing and Lee. Starting with re-boots of the *Frankenstein* and *Dracula* characters that put Universal at the forefront of horror films in the 1930's, Hammer was also responsible for stuffing Raquel Welch into a fuzzy bikini for *One Million Years BC*, released the same year as *Plague* (and also distributed stateside by 20th Century Fox). Although the studio was about to be trumped by a new legion of horror producers, both big-budget and small like Romero, this particular outing is lovingly regarded as one of Hammer's hidden gems. Well-scripted and acted with the usual decent level of skill displayed by a great many of Hammer's players, *Plague* is often referred to as the last great zombie flick before *Night of the Living Dead*.

As we've mentioned, director John Gilling was saddled with directing two films nearly at once on the backlots of Bray Studios in Britain—and fortunately for zombie fans, *The Reptile* was the flick that suffered. We've further mentioned that the same sets were used; heck, nearly the same *plot* was used for both films. Part of the reason *Plague* was a better movie had a lot to do with the snappy style of screenwriter Peter Bryan, who was responsible for the 1959 update of *The Hound of the Baskervilles*. Bryan, alas, was also behind Joan Crawford's last theatrical release, the unintentionally hilarious *Trog*.

The Plague of the Zombies Quiz
Answers on page 162.

Rating: DefCon 1

1. What unusual object is used as a candle holder?

Rating: DefCon 2

2. What type of hunting is practiced in the film?

Rating: DefCon 3

3. After making *The Plague of the Zombies*, director John Gilling and actor Andre Morell went on to make a mummy film for Hammer. What was its title?

Night of the Living Dead (1968)

When *Night of the Living Dead* opened in October of 1968, the MPAA's rating system was still a month away from implementation. This meant that kids as young as seven and eight years old attended matinee screenings of the movie—and are probably still in therapy as a result.

George Romero's *Night* is the standard-bearer for low-budget indie horror flicks. Scraped together on a budget just over $100,000, the film has pulled in close to $50 million worldwide. Romero and his cast and crew set the film in a rural town outside Pittsburgh, where Romero had studied at Carnegie Mellon University. Extras, responsible for perfecting the zombie stagger while wearing raccoon face paint and wounds constructed from mortician's wax, now find themselves signing autographs for fans of the movie at horror film conventions today.

The plot's fairly simple: A young woman named Barbra (Judith O'Dea) and her brother Johnny (an uncredited Russell Streiner) encounter a zombie in a cemetery while the pair are visiting their father's grave. After John is killed during a struggle with the monster, Barbra's panicked escape leads her to a farmhouse. Taking refuge there are quarreling marrieds and their daughter, a teenage couple, and an African-American man named Ben (Duane Jones)—who turns out to be the most rational of the bunch.

Zombies attack, survivors turn on one another, local newsmen advise the living to shoot zombies in the head, the little girl becomes a ghoul who uses her pop as an entrée—and all the while the 'doom factor' is pushed to its logical envelope masterfully by Romero's direction. Ultimately, Ben becomes the last man standing, living through the night only to be mistakenly taken for a zombie and shot—by an all-white posse.

Romero used a common convention found in B-movies from the era: radiation is a bad thing, and radiation from space is a REALLY bad thing. But in Romero's take, a dose of rays from space doesn't grow giant ants or monstrous Japanese lizards—the atomic particles re-animate the dead and leave 'em with a plodding need to dine on their neighbors. That's where the film departs from its sci-fi and horror predecessors: the monster is everywhere, and he—or she—looks a lot like us. With Goth makeup and a lousy tan, yeah, but still darn familiar.

The film's measly budget heightens the horror: *Night of the Living Dead* has the vibe of a wartime newsreel; grainy black-and-white footage, twitchy camera angles and lighting that runs from murky to interrogation-room washout. The newsy feel also harkened to images Americans were seeing every night on the evening news—the war in Vietnam was raging. Additionally, the not-so-friendly hero of the film was a black guy—a black guy who railed against the idiocy of his fellow white survivors only to be shot by a roving band of Caucasians. (Keep in mind that the film's release in the fall of '68 followed the fresh memory of the murder of Dr. Martin Luther King earlier that very year.)

Most critics hated the film, with a few notable exceptions including the legendary and influential Pauline Kael. She was in line with the general population, but Romero's new legion of fans would have to wait 10 years before George built a sequel—a sequel that was arguably better than his first.

Night of the Living Dead Quiz
Answers on page 163.

Rating: DefCon 1
1. How does Ben kill his first zombie in the film?

2. A satellite from what planet is said to be carrying the radiation?

3. Where is Cooper's daughter bitten?

4. True or False: *Night of the Living Dead* is on the National Film Registry.

Rating: DefCon 2
5. What does Ben say before he gets shot?

6. During her escape, how many times does Barbra fall?

7. News reports that the killers are eating the flesh of their victims. From where is that report coming?

Rating: DefCon 3
8. Star Duane Jones went on to head the theatre department at what college?

9. Another working title referenced the Egyptian god of mummification. What was that title and why was it dropped?

10. Bill 'Chilly Billy' Cardille played a TV reporter – for what did he became famous in his hometown of Pittsburgh?

George Romero Filmography Fill-In

Rating: DefCon 2

Below are the names of feature films directed by George Romero. Your task is to fill in the missing letters. Answers on page 163.

1. M O __ __ __ __   __ __ I N __ __

2. T H E   __ __ __ K   H __ __ __

3. __ __ __   __ __ __ Z __ __ __

4. __ N __ __ __ __ R __ __ __ __ __

5. __ __ __ __ __ __ __ __   __ __

   __ __ __   DEAD

6. __ __ __ T __ N

7. __ __ W __   __ __   __ __ __

   __ __ __ __

8. __ __ __   OF   __ __ __   __ __ __ D

9. __ R __ __ __ __ H __ __ __

Biography: George A. Romero

If there's one individual who can be pegged as the granddaddy of the modern zombie-movie genre, it's a ponytailed gent in his 70s with a penchant for eyeglasses as large as movie screens. The guiding hand and wildcat auteur who hobbled together a taut little film that changed the manner and style of B-movie horror forever is a chap named George Romero.

Born February 4, 1940, in the Big Apple, George Romero wound up at the same college that gave us Andy Warhol and Jack Klugman: Carnegie-Mellon University in Pittsburgh (CMU makes a notable location for the Hal Holbrook/Adrienne Barbeau vignette in Romero's *Creepshow*). Like a lot of kids who were growing up in 1950's America, Romero loved EC Comics titles such as *The Vault of Horror*, *The Haunt of Fear*, and *Tales from the Crypt* (do we really need to mention *Creepshow* again?), and before those books were driven into oblivion by the Comics Code Authority, millions of kids like Romero had already developed an appreciation of all things macabre. Lucky for us, Romero also got his hands on an 8mm camera at age 14, and filmmaking became his primary passion.

Horror wasn't George's stock-in-trade after college graduation, however—Romero began working on commercials for Pittsburgh products (Iron City Beer) and short segments for another Steel City production: *Mister Rogers' Neighborhood*. In the late '60s, Romero convinced some like-minded friends to chip in $10,000 apiece in order to create Image Ten Productions, the indie film startup built solely to produce a motion picture co-written by fellow Image Ten founder John A. Russo: a low-budget, B&W trifle entitled *Night of the Living Dead*. George had dug Richard Matheson's novel *I Am Legend* and a 1962 B-movie classic called *Carnival of Souls*, and he drew on those as inspiration along with his old comic books. Penning three short stories all about cannibalistic ghouls, Romero developed the first episode into his directorial debut. The premise was simple: dead people get up and walk—and eat the living, who turn into dead people, who get up and . . .

But, of course, the movie was much more than that: it was a newsreel-styled, angry-black-man-in the-lead, gory-as-hell-for-1968 knockout that audiences still find creepy, scary, and tragically moving. Lack of traditional means to steady the camera added to the fear—strange angles and wobbly shots keep the viewer as off-kilter as many of the frames. Families are dysfunctional, the average American appears to be fairly racist, bad behavior abounds in the face of the end times—and there's always a news report playing somewhere in the background. Not that George admires over-analysis of any of his films, mind you—Romero spoke wearily about fielding queries from horror-film-conventioneers to *Vanity Fair*'s Eric Spitznagel:

> *They've pulled apart every movie 50 ways from Sunday. Sometimes I just want to tell them, "Get a life, man! I had a great time making these films, but it doesn't sound like you're having as good a time watching them. You're getting too involved! Lighten up!"*

Romero and company couldn't have known that a bunch of extras staggering around in raccoon makeup and gnawing on hams covered in chocolate syrup (a joke on the set was that the actors didn't need pale-face zombie makeup since the ham and Bosco combo was already making 'em nauseous) would create an entire genre. Romero's first foray into zombie-moviedom established what are now well-known rules for zombie behavior—and execution. No more brain, no more zombie—"Shoot'em, beat 'em or burn 'em," to paraphrase Night's redneck sheriff.

The film had originally been titled *Night of the Flesh Eaters* (before that, its working moniker was *Monster Flick*) when Romero threw his reels in the trunk of his car and set off to find a distributor. After being nearly universally rejected (for everything from its gore to its black-and-white footage in the age when full color was considered a cinematic leg up on TV), the film finally found a distributor who casually changed the title. Romero wasn't trying to change cinema—he didn't consider himself a 'serious filmmaker' for years—he was simply trying to do what many 20-somethings have tried before, during and after the '60s: have a little fun and pay the rent. Romero's cavalier attitude about his first project allowed the movie to slip into the public domain—which meant that endless redistribution and countless creature-feature television screenings made Romero's title a household name and probably cost George millions.

Romero pressed on after *Night*, trying his hand at drama (*There's Always Vanilla*—his self-described worst) before returning to the macabre with varying success (*Season of the Witch, The Crazies*) and eventually shooting chapter two of his *Dead* series, *Dawn of the Dead*, a full-color classic that cemented his reputation as a horror master extraordinaire. *Dawn* also provided Romero with the opportunity to shoot a zombie movie with his pal, makeup and effects artist Tom Savini— Savini had been slated to handle the makeup on *Night*, but a tour in Vietnam prevented his participation.

Having shattered the idea of 'camp horror' when *Night* was released, Romero ironically visited the genre with 1982's aforementioned *Creepshow*, a joint venture with Stephen King that featured five vignettes, structured like the horror comics both men loved as kids. Romero returned to his zombie series with *Day of the Dead*, a film that received less critical acclaim than Romero's previous chapters, but the one that Romero loves best. Romero's technical skill, his storytelling ability and zombie-movie-as-political-statement would again be realized with spectacular results in *Land of the Dead*—made over 35 years after George first introduced us to his beloved ghouls. *Diary of the Dead* and *Survival of the Dead* continue the traditions laid out by Romero in 1968.

Children Shouldn't Play With Dead Things (1972)

Children Shouldn't Play with Dead Things is low-budget—really low-budget. Costs for Bob Clark's 1972 outing were reported to run anywhere from $50,000 to $70,000, and boy, it looks it. Overly lit, at times a challenge to hear and edited with what may have been a kindergartener's blunt-nose scissors and scotch tape, *Children* does mark another genre first for the man who went on to make both *Porky's* and *A Christmas Story*.

Children takes us along as the cruel, egomaniacal and eccentric Alan (Alan Ormsby) has brought the acting troupe he directs out to an island by boat. The island's a graveyard, and Al has a book of spells and a few tricks up his sleeve. He successfully convinces his employees—under constant threat of termination if they back out of Alan's fun and games—that he's brought two ghouls back to life. Nothing could be further from the truth; the undead turn out to be two other members of the group.

Alan's dug up a gent named Orville in order to use the coffin for the gag, and propping up the late Orville on a cross, Alan recites some spells from his book, intent on seeing if anything supernatural happens. Which, of course, it eventually does—the kids have busted into the caretaker's house, taking Orville along for laughs, and shortly several dozen hungry zombies are knocking at the door. The group gets picked off by twos after trying the old 'board up the doors' gambit, and eventually only Alan is left—alone in a room with the now re-animated Orville. Credits roll as the zombies find a boat to take them to the big city.

Children was shot in 11 days in Florida (where Clark had gone to college), and the lead in the film was integral in the production; Ormsby co-authored the flick and even handled some makeup chores. Alan was hitched to Anya (Anya Ormsby), a lithe little thing given to hysterics as the dead start creeping out of their graves. The dialogue ranges from witty to obnoxious as the actors zing one another and their various talents or lack thereof, and the whole production has a film-school-inside-joke feel to it. A lot of the actors also appeared in Clark's next horror show, *Dead of Night*, which was shot almost concurrently with *Children*.

The reason *Children Shouldn't Play With Things* is important is Clark himself—Bob Clark invented or re-invigorated genres time and time again. *Children* shows Clark getting his director's legs while creating the first true modern zombie comedy, and he'd go on to helm 1974's *Black Christmas*, a yarn about a killer knocking off sorority sisters credited in some circles as the beginning of the modern teen-slasher-movie era. Clark then singlehandedly created the teen-sex-comedy with *Porky's* and *Porky's 2*, films that allowed him to call a shot or two of his own in Hollywood—and led execs to back Clark's timeless and beloved collaboration with Jean Shepherd, 1983's *A Christmas Story*. (Clark appears in *Story* as Swede, the gent commenting on the Old Man's leg lamp as Darren McGavin admires his 'major award' from the street.)

After *Story* yielded a disappointing box office return, Clark's career began to lose steam with disappointing offerings like *Turk 182* (and another you'll find in the trivia quiz that follows). Clark had been attempting a comeback in the mid-2000's, however—he'd partnered with Howard Stern to begin work on a *Porky's* remake (which Clark based on some of his own coming-of-age experiences as a lad down south) and was in the planning stages for a re-boot of *Children* when Bob and his son Ariel were killed by a drunk driver in 2007.

Children Shouldn't Play With Dead Things includes a few other oddities: two of the male characters appear to be openly gay—maybe a first for horror flicks of this era—and if the voice of the rotund Jeff sounds familiar, close your eyes and think of *A Christmas Story*. Actor Jeff Gillen played the department store Santa who gives Ralphie a toe-tap to the forehead with the line, "You'll shoot your eye out, kid. Merry Christmas."

Children Shouldn't Play With Dead Things Quiz
Answers on page 163.

Rating: DefCon 1
1. What city are the corpses heading toward at the end of the film?

Rating: DefCon 2
2. What name is director Bob Clark billed as in *Children Shouldn't Play With Dead Things*?

Rating: DefCon 3
3. What Bob Clark film, starring Sylvester Stallone and Dolly Parton, earned him a Razzie Award?

Funny, You Don't Look Dead

Rating: DefCon 3

Match these horror comedies with their funny (or allegedly funny) stars. Answer on page 163.

Dead Heat	Bob Hope and Paulette Goddard
Beverly Hills Bodysnatchers	Treat Williams and Joe Piscopo
The Ghost Breakers	Vic Tayback and Frank Gorshin
Shaun of the Dead	Simon Pegg and Nick Frost

Working Out the Zombie Way

The dissection of zombie lore doesn't live solely in the halls of academe, to be sure. 2003's bestseller 'The Zombie Survival Guide', with its comic take on zombie-survival-methodology, had an underlying message that made it so wildly popular: self-reliance is key. A workout freak by the name of Rich Gatz heard that message loud and clear, and applied it to one of the most unique fitness regimens out there: 'ZombieFit'.

Gatz's parkour-style workout (billed as 'Fitness to Survive the Apocalypse'), expands on *Zombileand*'s First Rule of Zombie Survival (in the film, Rule # 1 is 'cardio'). Gatz's concept is expressed as 'performing functional movements at high intensity'. Just like parkour (as seen both on YouTube and a hilarious sequence from *The Office* TV series), the object of ZombieFit is to get from point A to point B as quickly as possible, using whatever's around to speed you on your way, whether it's walls, fire escapes, or stacks of corpses.

The notion here is that if you need to get away from an actual real-life bad guy, the best way is to learn how to get away from a supernatural bad guy. Says Gatz: "If you prepare for the impossible, you'll be ready for the improbable. If you spend three hours a day doing bicep curls in front of a mirror and running on a treadmill, all that prepares you for is doing bicep curls and running on a treadmill. By practicing parkour and actually learning functional movements at high intensity, you'll be able to run away from whoever it is you need to run away from." Fitness is, of course, a fringe benefit. "If you can run away from a horde of zombies, I bet you're gonna look pretty good, too."

Scrambled List

Rating: DefCon 1

Below is a list of objects that could be useful should you find yourself squaring off against a zombie. Just unscramble the letters to find the helpful goods. Solution on page 163.

1. SAELBBAL TBA   _____

2. THEECMA   _____

3. WASICHIN   _____

4. VOELHS   _____

5. GTHSONU   _____

6. DROWS   _____

7. ERIT NOIR   _____

Let Sleeping Corpses Lie (1974)

Spaniard Jorge Grau's *Let Sleeping Corpses Lie* took the fundamental elements of Romero's *Night of the Living Dead*—flesh-eating undead and a hefty dose of social commentary—and mixed in some fresh fears: science run amok, drug-addled hippies suspected of ritual murder . . . everything the headlines were screaming about in the early '70s.

George is a longhair from London. In an effort to get away from it all, he takes a few items from his art and antiques gallery in the city to his new home in the country. But the trip isn't all that relaxing: His motorbike is accidentally damaged by the lovely Edna, who's traveling to see her sister who lives in the boonies as well.

George needs a ride and is headed in Edna's general direction. Unfortunately, George and Edna get lost along the way, and as George hunts for a local with some geography knowledge, he stumbles across a group of technicians using sonic radiation to kill agricultural pests. Meanwhile, Edna's attacked by a madman—a gent who turns out to be a local loony named Guthrie who, we learn, has been dead for a week.

Guthrie kills a man, and the local reactionary police sergeant pegs the death on Edna's hollow-eyed junkie sister Katie—apparently drugs can make even the most fragile little gal kill with the strength of a dozen men. Sarge is equally convinced that freaks George and Edna may also be involved, and orders his suspects to hole up in the Old Owl Hotel, while Katie's sent to the local hospital—where three newborns have been attacking their nurses.

Eventually, a dead cop, crispy corpses (burning is the method of choice to eliminate these guys) and a wrecked graveyard leave ol' Sarge convinced that his lovely hamlet is being destroyed by a Manson-style Satanist creep. And poor George is now public enemy number one. (The antiques in his saddlebags, including some ancient African fertility symbols, don't help George's case much.)

Let Sleeping Corpses Lie builds the tension slowly before its zombies get down to full-color cannibalism. The film seems as influenced by Britain's Hammer films as by Romero's work—settings, makeup, a nod or two to vampirism all make one wonder if Christopher Lee might turn up at any moment. Shot in the UK, Rome and Spain, the original cut was voiced in Italian, and the cast is a truly international collection of nobodies.

Corpses also features something that was gaining popularity in the early '70s—gratuitous footage of naked female breasts. The film's opening sequence inexplicably includes a female streaker, and a later scene seems to suggest that male zombies like the fleshy bits of ladies for snacking as well. The gore, counterculture-versus-establishment, skin and ham-handed ecological message make *Corpses* an enduring cult film.

Theremins, organs and heavy breathing (handled by Grau himself) saturate the soundtrack, and though the film has a few problems—one zombie figures out how to run for about four seconds—it transitions nicely from lovely countryside to foggy nightmare.

Trivia note: The film's graveyard sequences were filmed at Heathersage, where Robin Hood's merry man 'Little John' is said to be buried.

Let Sleeping Corpses Lie Quiz

Answers on page 163.

Rating: DefCon 1

1. True or False: *Let Sleeping Corpses Lie* was also know as *The Living Dead at Manchester Morgue?*

2. True or False: *Let Sleeping Corpses Lie* was also known as *Don't Open the Door.*

Rating: DefCon 2

3. Nominated four times for Best-Supporting-Actor Oscars—although he never won—Arthur Kennedy plays the Sergeant in *Let Sleeping Corpses Lie*. In which of the following did he NOT appear?
   a. *Elmer Gantry*
   b. *They Died With Their Boots On*
   c. *Citizen Kane*
   d. *Peyton Place*
   e. The Broadway production of *Death of a Salesman*

Rating: DefCon 3

1. *Let Sleeping Corpses Lie* is also the name of a five-disc boxed set of music by what band?

Dawn of the Dead (1978)

It may be the best zombie movie ever shot—and maybe the best B movie of any genre, period. In spite of it status, recognition, box-office bite and staying power, George Romero's 1978 sequel to his black-and-white low budget hit *Night of the Living Dead* still has one critical flaw: Who's keeping the power on during a month-long zombie apocalypse?

Okay, okay, all wonkiness aside, *Dawn of the Dead* represents a high-water mark for splatter-films on a shoestring. Made for $650,000 during the winter of 1977-1978, (it's raked in well over $55 million) *Dawn* takes everything Romero learned about character development, critiquing American society and making human heads explode and amps it up to 11—this time in color. The film became an instant cult classic, replayed for years in midnight showings all over America.

Romero's *Dawn* begins in a television station where chaos is reigning. Commentators and crew are struggling to get the right information to the public in the midst of a grisly event in which the dead have begun to feed on the living. The TV's chopper pilot, Stephen (David Emge), is planning to bug out with Fran (Gaylen Ross), another employee of WGON-TV. On the air, an announcement is made that private residences aren't considered safe—they're being cleared by the authorities.

Cleared is an understatement. In the projects, a SWAT team and a National Guard unit are fighting a group of residents who have no use for martial law. One cop uses the pretext of insurrection as the perfect excuse to wipe out anyone with a darker skin tone than his, and does so gleefully, his attacks peppered with vile ethnic slurs. The dead are being stowed in the basement of the building, and coming back to life to feast on whoever's about. Two members of the SWAT team, Roger (Scott H. Reiniger) and Peter (Ken Foree) , have stumbled upon the zombies, and Peter—an African American gent, by the way—resignedly executes the zombies with his pistol.

To this point, Romero's already built a classic; this isn't just what a zombie apocalypse looks like, it's what fearful anarchy *feels* like. Some cling to the vestiges of a civilization being wiped out—for example, a TV exec doesn't give a damn about broadcasting correct info as long as the station holds to its ratings strategy—but the four central characters realize that all bets are off and the air is the only safe place. Roger invites Peter to join Stephen and Fran, and soon Stephen's bird is in the air.

The survivors drift west, passing over the hills where rednecks are hunting the walking dead with a creepy beer-sodden joy. Eventually a shopping mall comes into view on the horizon—and this where the bulk of the action takes place. The four land at the mall, currently populated by zombies who've returned out of habit or some deep memory of consumer happiness, and begin to set up shop. Zombies tread past the shops and up the escalators to the strains of abysmal late-70s canned music, while the survivors raid the various stores for goods and wipe out the undead mall-walkers inside the shopping center.

An attempt to barricade the mall's entrances with trucks results in a couple of nasty bites for Roger, who begins a slow slide toward death, shots of morphine from Fran his only comfort. Roger promises to try and stay dead once the inevitable happens, but in the end his reanimated corpse is rendered lifeless with a bullet delivered by Peter. The three that remain settle in as days pass, arming themselves, furnishing a series of storerooms and offices into a hidden apartment. Pregnant Fran has begun to show when the mall is targeting by a band of bikers—they want in, they want food and they want the goodies in Penny's and the gun shop.

The bikers engage the ghouls with firearms, hatchets and custard—yep, there's a human/zombie pie fight in this one—and more than one biker is hungrily disemboweled by the armies of the undead. Stephen succumbs to an attack and leads the monsters to the hiding place, forcing Fran (who's learned how to fly the chopper) and Peter to run.

Peter's decision to escape doesn't come easily—he contemplates suicide first; in fact, an alternate ending to the film called for Peter to put a bullet in his brain and Fran to jam her skull into the whirling blades of the helicopter (this too is an effective zombie-killing device, as we learn early in the film). Romero ultimately decided that killing everybody for a second straight zombie film was simply too depressing.

Dawn of the Dead is loaded with merry potshots at American culture—it's reported that Romero got the idea while visiting a mall and saw the blissful looks on the faces of the shoppers. One of the early zombie attackers in the mall is a lumbering Hare Krishna, complete with shaven head and tambourine, a blind follower of his . . . urges? Religion? The over-the-top violence of the early portion of the film is loaded with racial conflict, but later scenes become more introspective in the way they probe what we're about: is it worth bringing a new life into this disaster? Has the complete breakdown of everything rendered any kind of human intimacy an empty exercise?

Romero, who had shot everything from low budget horror flicks to Iron City beer commercials, was recovering financially from the failure of a film called *Season of the Witch* and the middling success of *The Crazies* when he scraped together the funding for *Dawn*. The shopping center scenes were filmed overnights at Monroeville Mall outside Pittsburgh, once one of the largest malls in America. Shooting ended every morning not when the doors opened, but when the actual muzak came on in the mall—nobody could figure out how to turn it off. Romero also suspended shooting for the Christmas shopping season.

Since Romero had little budget for stuntmen, makeup and effects wizard Tom Savini was pressed into service in between improvising horrible wounds and shipping in cow intestines to double for human ones. Savini was never happy with the bluish tint of the undead or the brilliant crimson of the faux blood he'd concocted; Romero, however, loved it, feeling that it harkened back to the gore he so fondly remembered from the pages of the old EC comic books. Romero also loved star David Emge's zombie walk as the undead version of Stephen, but he handed the most memorable line in zombie-film history to Peter: "When there's no more room in hell, the dead will walk the Earth."

Dawn of the Dead Quiz
Answers on page 163.

Rating: DefCon 1
1. From what city do the broadcasts in the beginning of the film emit?

Rating: DefCon 2
2. Some of the cyclists were played by members of what actual motorcycle club/gang?

Rating: DefCon3
3. George Romero also shot for what long-running children's TV show?

Zombi 2/Zombie (1979)

Whether it's Westerns, skin flicks or zombie movies, the Italians really, really like to try their hand at American genres.

Shortly after Romero's *Dawn of the Dead* made its way overseas, Roman Lucio Fulci—who later earned the title 'Godfather of Gore'— released *Zombi 2* to international infamy. (*Dawn* was entitled *Zombi* in Italy; the two are unrelated otherwise). The flick made the former med student a horror legend.

Fulci's *Zombi 2* (or simply *Zombie* in its US release) begins with a sailing vessel drifting into New York's harbor. Cops board the boat to find some rotting food—and an incredibly fat undead fellow who proceeds to turn one of the policemen into snack food. The boat was the property of the father of one Anne Bowles (Tisa Farrow, proving that sister Mia got all the acting chops in the family), and there's a letter aboard from father to daughter. Anne teams up with a reporter (Peter West, played by Ian McCulloch) who's on the case of the murdered cop. Since the boat was last heard from when it was sailing the Antilles, the pair head south to find out what happened to Pop.

They meet up with a couple named Brian and Susan, two Americans who have a boat and are willing to drop them on Mr. Bowles's favorite hangout, a rumor-has-it-to-be-cursed island called Matool. (Matul? Matoul? No matter. It's uncharted.) Matool's primary features are a) poverty, b) wildly stereotypical locals and c) a doctor named Menard who runs a ramshackle hospital and tries to keep his smokin' hot wife Paola from drinking all the whiskey in the Caribbean.

As our four at-sea adventurers head toward Matool, Susan decides to go for a dip to take some underwater photos. Susan's scuba wear of choice includes little more than a tank, flippers and a g-string, which make her all the more appetizing for the male viewer—and the shark and the zombie waiting below. What follows is the film's most demented sequence: shark threatens girl, zombie threatens girl, then shark and zombie start gnawing on each other. (The actor who was originally slated to battle the shark was sick that day—who wouldn't be?—and the animal's trainer stood in.) Susan escapes with her boobies fully intact, but the shark rams the boat and screws up the driveshaft. (Yes, *Zombi 2* was scripted after *Jaws* was released.)

Back on Matool, as disease grips the island, Mrs. Menard is taking a shower (Fulci's supporting actresses seemed to be cast primarily for their looks without a shirt) when the zombies come calling. Paola is dispatched with the old splinter-in-the-eye trick, which is nauseously, horribly, painstakingly depicted. The boat limps into Matool, our crew meets up with Menard, and the good Doctor asks the group to check in on his wife while Menard gets back to the business of shooting corpses in the head at his third-world health care facility. Our group witnesses a gang of ghouls munching on Paola and hustle down the trail, only to wreck their car and attempt to make it back to the hospital on foot.

Alas, a voodoo curse has begun to overspread the island, and the dead are poppin' up all over. Susan meets her end in a cemetery full of Spanish conquistadors who've held up pretty nicely in tropical conditions for 400 years, thank you very much. The three survivors stagger back to the hospital where they make their final stand against the legions of the undead. Menard is taken down, as is his nurse and Haitian assistant, and Peter, Anne and Brian escape to Brian's boat—but not before a re-animated Susan gives Brian a fatal hickey. Anne and Peter sputter away with zombie Brian locked below while the radio broadcasts some really bad news from the Big Apple—seems NYC is in about the same shape as Matool.

Although the acting is truly awful, and some 'mood-building' shots drag on at length, Fulci's grindhouse blasts of visual goop make for some pretty terrific sequences. Blood flows freely and more than a few zombie nibbles are portrayed in all their grisly glory. Zombie actors are caked with mud, blood and crud (Fulci referred to his extras as 'walking flower pots'), and many of them have worms wriggling about on their lips as they rise from the earth. Fulci's not afraid of the subjective camera, either—there's something strangely beautiful about seeing the sunlight the way a zombie might after decades underground.

Fulci had helmed everything from Spaghetti-Westerns to political satires before he hit his stride with horror in the late '70s and '80s. Fulci was a contemporary of Dario Argento (*Suspiria*) and the two sometime-rivals were working on a project together when Fulci passed suddenly from diabetes-related factors in 1987. Critics are split on whether Fulci was a maestro of the macabre or just a skingoria pornographer (the right answer is 'all of the above').

Zombi 2/Zombie Quiz

Answers on page 164.

Answers on page 164.

Rating: DefCon 1

1. True or false: The English-language poster for the movie declared "We are going to eat you!"

Rating: DefCon 2

2. What was handed out to theatergoers attending the film in the U.S.?

Rating: DefCon 3

3. Director Roman Lucio Fulci makes a cameo as what?

Solution on page 170.

Across

1. Big bash at Zombie Film Feast (should this be fest?)
5. Snatches
10. Horror directors Bohus and Mikels
14. Barely manages, with "out"
15. Unit of money used to make Bollywood zombie films
16. Letters of urgency, concerning a zombie attack
17. With 66-Across, 1968 classic directed by George A. Romero (3 wds.)
19. In the buff, like a naked zombie
20. Starfleet Academy grad.
21. Long gun used in zombie killing
22. Quarterfinals or semifinals
23. Gathering of horror film fans: Zombie ___
24. Site to search for zombie movies
26. Places to play "Spooksville" and "Scared Stiff" pinball machines
30. Small amount
31. La-la preceder
34. 1972 chiller, ___ *Dead Delilah*
35. "The butler ___ it"
37. Lead male character of 17-Across
39. Blast from the past
41. Raven's beak
43. Poke fun at a zombie
44. Lead female character of 17-Across
46. Historical period
48. Bearing
49. John Fogerty tune: "___ of the Zombie"
50. *Dead ___ Buried*
52. Calgary's province
54. Willow for wicker
56. Home for a group of werewolves
57. 2005 video game based on scare flick, "___ in the Dark"

60. Monster escapade
62. *I Was a Zombie for the* ___ (1982)
65. Wise men
66. See 17-Across (2 wds.)
68. Norwegian city in *Lake of the Dead*
69. Highly skilled, like zombie hunters
70. "___ in the coffin"
71. Razor-sharp
72. Monster brawl
73. Like many student zombie films

Down

1. Star of *Young Frankenstein*, ___ Wilder
2. Blood-related
3. Limbs cut off in trimmed scenes from *Friday the 13th, Part 3*
4. Volcanic fallout
5. To build with intersecting vaults
6. Dennis the Menace's dog
7. In a fitting way
8. Execute a zombie in old France
9. Get an eyeful
10. It's a no-no
11. Jacob's biblical twin
12. Sock-mender's oath?
13. Hightailed it from the cemetery
18. Crushed underfoot, as Godzilla in Tokyo
22. Automaton, like Yul Brynner in *Westworld*
23. West Indies native
25. Pilgrimage to Mecca
26. Pueblo brick
27. Pass-the-baton race
28. Band of zombies fighters
29. Film from Frank Miller graphic novel: ___ *City*
31. TV studio sign (2 wds.)
32. Get-go
33. "Laughing" scavenger
36. What immortals never do

38. Skeletor's nemeses
40. Remove a zombie movie from a tape
42. Janet Leigh's lingerie item in *Psycho*
45. Start of an Indiana University cheer: "Gimme ___!" (2 wds.)
47. Italian for "to the tooth" (2 wds.)
51. Make up one's mind about a zombie
53. Ice formation where monster sits at end of Mary Shelly's novel
54. Humor newspaper (with "The") that ran "Zombie Nutritionist Recommends All-Brain Diet" headline
55. Become unwoven

57. With wild abandon, like zombies on the loose
58. Use a surgical beam
59. Eyeball lustfully, a la Peter Lorre
61. Lead weapon used to bash Michael Myers in the head in *Halloween 6*
62. Cause of cold sweat
63. Can of worms?
64. One way to stand by
66. Hasty escape by a zombie
67. Genetic stuff extracted from dinosaur fossils in *Jurassic Park*

Dead and Buried (1981)

Dead and Buried suffers from two major problems: some pretty dreadful acting by the supporting cast and antiquated film stock and dubbing techniques that make some scenes seem only slightly more advanced than the average college-project shoot. The saving grace here is the screenplay—in fact, the distributors knew it and included in the film's poster that it originated from the 'creators of *Alien*'. Ron Shusett and Dan O'Bannon, the men who'd penned the iconic sci-fi/horror epic, adapted a story by Alex Stern and Jeff Millar—this seems to be Stern's one and only film credit; Millar had little more than *ABC Afterschool Specials* under his belt.

The film opens with a photographer visiting the seaside town of Potter's Bluff. He's shooting waves, birds, boats—and shortly a cute blonde with some pretty loose morals shows up in his frame. She poses for the camera, flashes some skin, propositions the shooter—and without warning the poor guy sees his afternoon turn from awesome to awful. A gaggle of townsfolk appear, and half are interested in photographing the poor sap while the other half are intent on burning him alive.

The locals stuff their victim into his VW Microbus and set up an 'accident' scene—they're trying to make it appear that the photog met his end in a flaming wreck. The local sheriff (played by TV staple James Farentino) and the town mortician (Jack Albertson in a serious departure from such roles as the small-screen curmudgeon in *Chico and the Man*) soon discover that the crash victim is clinging to life. After depositing the poor photographer in the hospital, another stranger is murdered, and it's not long before the Sheriff realizes that Potter's Bluff is getting to be kind of dangerous.

As Sheriff Gillis garners more and more evidence that something in town is really amiss, his wife's behavior becomes stranger and stranger—she seems to be interested in voodoo and witchcraft, and her absences from the Gillis home become more and more difficult to explain. Additionally, those who have passed on begin to turn up—in fine shape, mind you—walking and talking and acting like completely normal residents of Potter's Bluff.

Dead and Buried plays more like sci-fi/crime drama than horror film, in fact, it really owes a lot more to *The Stepford Wives* or *Westworld* than *Night of the Living Dead*. These zombies aren't lumbering, monosyllabic types—and there's also some actual character arcs here, too. The Sheriff's wife Jan (Melody Anderson), initially suspect #1 in the viewer's mind, rapidly becomes a much more sympathetic figure—even though the Sheriff will stumble across a reel of film starring Jan that sums up the evil secret that the town secretly holds.

While the bloody bits are few and far between, the ones that remained in the final cut caused controversy: a needle in an eyeball, a doctor's acid-infused melting face and the reconstruction of the head of an expired hitchhiker brought a bit of infamy to this low-budget creeper. Shot in Mendocino, CA—a nice double for the scripted New England coastal setting if you ignore certain types of vegetation—the look of this picture is appropriately foggy and dark. The pacing's hit or miss, some of the transitions are downright weird, but the notion, the basic premise of the flick and the ending—which might well have been stolen by M. Night Shyamalan—make for a pretty satisfying experience by the time the end credits roll.

The shoot was a struggle for the beloved Jack Albertson. Playing a creepy mortician behind bottle-thick lenses, Albertson was suffering from the advance of cancer during the making of *Dead and Buried*, in fact, this became Jack's last theatrical release. Moreover, the idea of *Willy Wonka*'s sympathetic grandfather presiding over a town full of zombies and a collection of snuff films adds to the cringe factor.

Dead and Buried Quiz
Answers on page 164.

Rating: DefCon 1

1. Harry, one of Potter's Bluff's murderous residents is played by Robert Englund. Three years later, what horror movie icon would Englund play?

Rating: DefCon 2

2. Melody Anderson, who played the sheriff's wife, also played heroine Dale Arden in the big-screen remake of what famous science fiction movie serial?

Rating: DefCon 3

3. Dan O'Bannon also wrote and directed what 1985 zombie film starring Clu Gulager?

The Evil Dead (1981)

You don't really watch Sam Raimi's *The Evil Dead*, you *endure* it for 85 minutes. Its subhead: "The Ultimate Experience in *Grueling* Horror!"

Shot starting in 1979 with a working budget of $375, 000, Rami's first feature-length horror show is a terrific mashup of demon-possession/zombie/kill-'em-off-one-by-one slasher films that's generated a huge cult following worldwide—even in places like Finland and Germany where the film was originally banned.

The set-up couldn't be more cliché: Five college kids go off into the woods for a weekend getaway, driving over a bridge that's about to collapse as ominous shadows flicker in the woods. The old cabin they're staying in has a cellar door that likes to pop open by itself. Venturing downstairs, the two males in the group, Ash and Scott, find a dagger topped by a skull, a reel-to-reel tape deck, and a strange book filled with hieroglyphics and drawings of skulls. Upon flipping on the tape deck, the kids realize they're renting the abandoned home of an archeologist who conveniently left behind a recorded explanation of the book—it's a nasty little how-to manual (with a cover made of human skin, natch) on waking sleeping demons who possess and then zombie-fy their human hosts.

Despite the protests of Ash's sister Cheryl, Scott skips ahead in the tape to some strange chanting, and the kids soon realize that mixing a rotten travel agent and Sumerian incantations makes for a terrible vacation.

Ultimately, Cheryl is, ahem, *violated* by the woods themselves and winds up stuffed in the cellar as she becomes more and more revolting. Once possessed, a human host who's then killed—and this flick covers every possible way to off your fellow demonically controlled BFF—becomes a 'deadite', a zombie who can only be stopped by dismemberment. Deadites don't seem as hungry as your run-of-the-mill zombie; sure, they'll gnaw on your shins, but they're far more interested in recruiting more of the living to their team.

Another difference from standard zombie fare: That creature in the basement doesn't just want to eat our heroes and recruit more undead, it also talks trash. Being eaten is bad, being teased by your eater is even worse.

Eventually, Ash discovers that everyone's got to be killed and cut up—his sister, his girlfriend, his buddy, everybody—but that the quickest way to get rid of all of 'em completely is to burn the book. All of 'em, that is, except for that one nasty critter who creeps up just as the credits roll . . .

The Evil Dead is notable for its stylistic originality—the thing plays like an acid-infused nightmare—and the absolute torrents of gore that drip from the humans, the Deadites, even the electrical outlets of the house. This film is so messy that star Bruce Campbell—'Ash'—often rode home from a day's shooting in the bed of a pickup truck. Fake blood does terrible things to a car's interior.

Raimi was a big fan of the Three Stooges and used quite of bit of Stooge-like choreography in his first feature, which adds to the general trippiness of the production. (Imagine a classic Mo Howard eye-poke taken to its logical conclusion.) Additionally, stand-ins are credited as 'fake shemps' in the end credits. Sam is never afraid to turn the camera sideways or even upside-down to heighten the horror, and although the climactic Deadite meltdown is as crude-looking today as the stop-motion effects used in a Rankin-Bass Christmas special, the overall impact is still as shocking as it was in the early '80s. (Bugs, corn syrup—and is that *tapioca?*—make for marvelous zombie innards.)

The Evil Dead Quiz

Answers on page 164.

Rating: DefCon 1

1. Which of the Coen Brothers (of *Fargo* and *True Grit* fame), was assistant editor on *The Evil Dead*?

2. True or False: *The Evil Dead* was Bruce Campbell's first feature film.

Rating: DefCon 2

3. What sort of Demons are released by the reading of the Necronomicon?

4. After making *The Evil Dead*, *Evil Dead II*, *Darkman*, and *Army of Darkness*, director Sam Rami landed a gig directing what western?

Rating: DefCon 3

6. Cheryl says "Kill me if you can _____." (Hint: It's the name of a rock group)

7. In what state was *The Evil Dead* shot?

Michael Jackson's *Thriller* (1983)

A video costing half a million dollars? Shot on 25 mm? Helmed by an A-list director? And running 14 minutes?

Maybe you had to have been there. But the hoopla surrounding Michael Jackson's *Thriller*—the album, the song, and to the point here, the video—was unprecedented.

Keep in mind that the music video business was still young. Sure, there had been short films based on songs before, but MTV made visuals a key component in pop music when it launched in 1981.

And it may be difficult for today's diversified audience to understand just how big Michael Jackson was at the time. Sure, he had limited experience as an actor (The scarecrow in the tanked big-screen adaptation of *The Wiz* was pretty much the extent of it) but from the moment he moonwalked to "Billie Jean" on the Motown 25th Anniversary TV special, he became the most popular entertainer on the planet. Jackson not only cracked MTV's largely whites-only entertainment lineup, he dominated it with "Billie Jean" and "Beat It" on frequent rotation.

Then he made a call to director John Landis, best known for *Animal House* but whose *An American Werewolf in London* had a mix of fun and scary that appealed to Jackson. They enlisted make-up legend Rick Baker to create a cat-like monster from Jackson's distinct features.

The plot: Young couple is on a date. Car breaks down. Young man informs his lady that he is different and, when the full moon arrives, he transforms into a kind of feline version of a werewolf. Ah, but it's only a movie, being watched by Michael and a date. A little freaked out, she leaves the theater. Their walk takes them past a cemetery where the dead come to life. The young man turns into one of them and the ghouls dance. He continues his pursuit of the girl who—surprise!—wakes up from a dream. But a look to the camera reveals that Michael sill has those creepy yellow eyes.

As the credits roll, the zombies dance back to their not-quite-final resting places.

Hey, nobody said it was *Citizen Kane*.

But the flick did go on to win a Grammy for Best Long Form Video and become the first music video to be included in the Library of Congress' National Film Registry.

And it's still a kick—which can't be the same for Jackson's follow-up, the lame science fiction 3-D short *Captain Eo* (directed by Francis Ford Coppola).

Thriller Quiz

Answers on page 164.

Rating: DefCon 1

   1. What horror movie icon voiced the rap section of "Thriller" and appeared as a zombie at the end of the video?

Rating: DefCon 2

   2. Michael Jackson's co-star, Ola Ray, was best know before *Thriller* as a model for what magazine?

Rating: DefCon 3

   3. What are the two primary colors in Jackson's letterman's jacket in *Thriller*?

Musical Interlude: Zombie Musicals

While we can't recall their presence in a Broadway musical, zombies have broken out in song in a number of campy off-Broadway and regional live stage shows.

With productions in cities as far flung as Tokyo, Japan, Grapevine, Texas, Toronto and New York, the most popular of these may be *Evil Dead: The Musical*.

Launched in the back room of a Montreal bar in 2003, the show made it to off-Broadway in 2006, complete with a first-few-rows "splatter zone" and an original cast recording.

Thanks to the latter, it's now possible for fans to groove on such tunes as "Cabin in the Woods," "Do the Necronomicon," and the classic "All the Men in My Life Keep Getting Killed by Candarian Demons" before they even get to the theater.

A decade before *Evil Dead: The Musical*, though, there was *Zombie Prom*. Launched in 1993 in Key West, the show also made it to off-Broadway (in 1996), and led to a 36-minute film version featuring RuPaul. In it, teenage rebel Jonny returns from the dead, causing an uproar at Enrico Fermi High over whether or not he should be allowed to attend the big dance.

Since those, there have been an invasion of shows, including *Zombie! The Musical*, *Z: A Zombie*, and *Chomp: a Zombie Musical*.

C.H.U.D. (1984)

Whether the purists among us call them zombies or simply radioactive mutants, the title critters in *C.H.U.D.*—short for 'Cannibalistic Underground Humanoid Dwellers'—sure act like the ghouls we've come to know. They swarm and feed on human flesh! They're kinda tough to kill—unless you take off the head! They're accompanied by a script that must have been full of exclamation points!

C.H.U.D. is a low-budget mess of a movie that saves the bucks on special effects with a device that creature-feature producers of '50s monster epics often used: show the creepy rubber hand (claw?), show the choppers and the glowing eyes, then cut away during the actual bloodletting. What do we get? Reactions from those listening in! Victims pulled into tunnels! Shots without any light! Add a soundtrack that's cheesier than the biggest block of Velveeta, layer in lots and lots of screaming, some cops, barrels of toxic waste, and you've got a flick that really owes more to the drive-in than George Romero.

Shot in New York City in the pre-Seinfeld/pre-Giuliani era, *C.H.U.D.* goes out of its away to paint the Big Apple as a dump. (Literally. More on that later.) Soho, shown here just before the gentry began shoving out the Starving Artists, is a mecca for the homeless. They live underground, their only food provided by a 'Reverend' named A.J. (Daniel Stern—yep, *that* Daniel Stern). Their comings and goings have been documented by a sympathetic photographer named Cooper (John Heard—yep, *that* John Heard) who's moved to the neighborhood with his main squeeze Lauren (Kim Greist right before she landed the role of Jill Layton, the dream girl in *Brazil*). A.J. is visited by Police Captain Bosch (Christoper Curry—nope, we haven't heard of him either) in his soup kitchen—seems there's a rash of missing persons in the neighborhood. A.J.'s homeless flock is dwindling, and the Captain's wife has gone missing, too.

A reporter is trying to figure out what's got the cops so busy of late, A.J. and Bosch are trying to figure out why the Nuclear Regulatory Commission's annual sweep (really? Annual sweep?) is taking an unusually long time to inspect Soho's sewers, and before long, we get a glimpse of what's been gnawing on everybody: MUTANT HOMELESS PEOPLE WITH BIG FANGS AND GLOWING EYES! played by LUMBERING EXTRAS IN HILARIOUS RUBBER SUITS! As our various heroes—photographer, 'Reverend', reporter and cop—try to figure out what's going on under the streets, we begin to realize that IT'S ALL A GOVERNMENT PLOT TO DUMP TOXIC WASTE UNDER MANHATTAN—RESULTS BE DAMNED! engineered by an evil bureaucrat named Wilson (George Martin). Soon enough, we learn that the acronym *C.H.U.D.* stands for something far more sinister . . .

C.H.U.D. is so awesomely bad it's, well, awesome. So derivative that it even includes a bloody scene in which the lead blonde takes a shower as a ghoul approaches, *C.H.U.D.* ultimately feels like a project ripped from multiple thrillers—there's devices lifted from *Alien*, the *Living Dead* series, even *Jaws*. (Curry and Stern claim that the original script was even worse, and they were heavily involved in re-writes during shooting.) Sloppy editing (especially ironic since director Douglas Cheek made the better part of his living as a film cutter) and a weird sense of continuity make for a nearly surreal experience—and yet the film's Grade-Z sci-fi Eisenhower-era-throwback vibe is ultimately charming.

There's another aspect to *C.H.U.D.* that makes for fun viewing—you'll probably recognize everybody in this number who's not wearing a rubber suit. Daniel Stern and John Heard would work together again in the first two *Home Alone* films—Heard played the dad and Stern played Joe Pesci's bad-guy partner—and Christopher Curry played a cop in the awful third installment of that series after Macauly Culkin had left. *C.H.U.D.*'s now a cult classic, and even spawned an even-worse-sequel, which has more of a traditional zombie-film plot.

C.H.U.D. Quiz
Answers on page 164.

Rating: DefCon 1
1. What *Roseanne* cast member has a small role as a cop flirting with a waitress?

Rating: DefCon 2
2. John Heard was menaced by a feline Nastassja Kinski in what 1982 horror film?

Rating: DefCon 3
3. Name the sequel to *C.H.U.D.*

Name the Actor

Answers on page 164.

Rating: DefCon 2

1. The actor who appeared in the 1985 movie *House*—which included a zombie among its many domestic horrors—also played "The Greatest American Hero" in the TV show of the same name.

2. An actor in the back-from-the-dead officer film *Maniac Cop* also starred in *The Evil Dead*.

3. The leader of a boat full of the living dead in *Pirates of the Caribbean: The Curse of the Black Pearl* also starred in the movie *Shine*.

4. An actor who appeared in *Pet Sematary* also starred in the TV show *The Munsters*.

5. The star of the *Resident Evil* films also played Joan of Arc in *The Messenger*.

6. The star of *The Serpent and the Rainbow* also played Meg Ryan's would-be husband in *Sleepless in Seattle*.

7. The star of *Shanks* also had the only spoken word in Mel Brooks' *Silent Movie*.

8. The star of *The Supernaturals* also played the lead in *Grease 2*.

9. The star of *Warning Sign* is perhaps best known as the star of TV's *Law and Order*.

10. A star of *Zombie Nightmare* is best known as TV's *Batman*.

Re-Animator (1985)

Stuart Gordon's *Re-Animator* is a throwback of sorts; at its heart lays a romance—a romance doomed in classic gothic fashion. This cult classic takes the 'Frankenstein' premise (Gordon felt that there were too many darn vampire movies around at the time) and expands it with madness and multiplication. Hey, if the good doctor imagined by Mary Shelley and James Whale could re-animate a corpse and then give him an undead bride, why not resurrect kitties and burn victims, too?

Re-Animator understands a few critical things that some flicks miss: a film needs a rhythm, even if it's a rhythm applied to nudity and gore; bright light can be as creepy as the dark, and hospitals are bloody scary—and just plain bloody, too. The movie also understands tension—it builds in an almost, well, literary fashion. *Re-Animator*, especially the available uncut DVD version, offers disembodied brains and boobies in a way that never seems terribly gratuitous by modern standards, then layers on a sense of humor so dark and subtle it demands a few viewings to catch all the jokes.

Herbert West (fan fave Jeffrey Combs) has been studying with Swiss doctor Hans Gruber (no, not the conductor, and no, not Alan Rickman's bad guy in *Die Hard*). After Gruber kicks during an experiment gone very wrong, the morbidly creepy Herbert enrolls at Miskatonic U in Massachusetts, where he rooms with promising student Dan—who happens to be knockin' boots with the Dean's daughter, Megan. Herbie and Dan are taught by the pompous plagiarist Dr. Carl Hill, played with gleeful malevolence by the long-faced David Gale. Doc Hill has it in for West, who challenges him at every turn, and he's got a very creepy crush on Megan to boot.

Herbert, you see, has a serum—a serum he's developed from research initially undertaken by the late Gruber—that re-animates human tissue. He proves the efficacy of the drug on Dan's dead cat, and before long Herbie and Dan are sneaking into the morgue to bring humans back from beyond. Discovered in the act by Dean Halsey, a violent zombie attacks the Dean, and our dynamic duo bring the good Dean back from the dead as well.

The evil Hill, having pinched Gruber's work, now sets his sights on ripping off Herbert and taking the credit. Herbert neatly beheads the bad Doctor with a shovel, and, ever the researcher, West brings both the head and the body back to life. His actions only lead to a really cranky corpse who likes to carry his head around in a pan—Hill spends the rest of the picture literally in pieces. His body's still strong—very strong, in fact, it's a side effect of Herbert's glowing drugs—and his mind is still twisted. Hill's developed a laser lobotomy procedure that can make the undead his minions—including Megan's pop, Dean Halsey.

The headless Hill's attempt to copulate with the ivory-skinned Megan (remember the multiple entendres regarding the word 'head'), the zombie platoon at the Doctor's command, Herbert's incessant need to continue his medical experiments in the face of utter mayhem—none of it overshadows the heartfelt tragedy of love lost between Dan and Megan. Somehow amidst all the bone-saws and straitjackets, Gordon manages to re-set the central relationships of the film: it's all about love and jealously. And intestines, too.

Re-Animator's cult status may have much to do with its utterly black sense of humor, something that was telegraphed brilliantly by some of the film's marketing. One tagline for the flick read: 'Herbert West has a good head on his shoulders. And another on his desk.' Jeff Comb's portrayal of West—the creepy cackle, the 'I am a scientist' delivery of his lines, and pores as big as potholes make for a perfect med-student gone mad. *Re-Animator*'s witty and taut structure helped it recoup its modest budget of $900,000—one hopes the producers didn't shell out too much for the score. You'll notice in the credits that the music was performed by the Rome Philharmonic Orchestra—we imagine the composer probably hoped that the Italians wouldn't notice how heavily he'd borrowed from Bernard Hermann's overture for Hitchcock's *Psycho*.

Re-Animator Quiz
Answers on page 165.

Rating: DefCon 1
1. *Re-Animator* is very loosely based on a story by what legendary horror writer?

Rating: DefCon 2
2. Which is longer, the original R-rated version or the unrated version?

Rating: DefCon 2
3. Name one of the two sequels to *Re-Animator*.

Day of the Dead (1985)

Although it didn't have the same impact as *Dawn of the Dead*, *Day of the Dead* is a taut film, in fact, it's Romero's favorite. The third in George's *Living Dead* series, *Day of the Dead* opens with a nod to the end of *Dawn*—four characters are hunting for survivors in a chopper. The action's moved to Florida, and the airborne group are mostly civilians—a Doctor named Sarah, a Jamaican pilot named John, a radio tech and a soldier named Miguel who's clearly suffering from post-zombie-apocalypse-stress-disorder.

They're hunting for survivors, but all they find are creeping undead and newspapers announcing the zombie attacks. Cars are abandoned, useless wads of cash flutter in the breeze, and palm trees sway—we're close to the Caribbean origin of zombie mythology. Forced back into their aircraft, they fly to their bunker—a scientific operation guarded by a small band of soldiers who have just lost their commander. The military, much like nature, abhors a vacuum; the nearly-psychotic Captain Rhodes is now in charge.

The operation centers around the work of a Doctor Logan and his team—the doc, not-so-lovingly referred to as 'Frankenstein' by the troops, is trying to figure out what makes those darn zombies tick. He's cutting them up and putting 'em back together in a most gory fashion. The good doctor's experiments, in fact, have led him to discover a reanimated corpse he calls 'Bub'. Bub's a zombie with a heart of gold—he doesn't immediately attempt to gnaw on Logan when the doctor approaches. He remains calmly chained to the wall, displaying a memory of objects such as toothbrushes and books (a Stephen King paperback prop here—Romero and King are pals). Bub even attempts to use a telephone properly—he's Romero's only zombie to have a line of dialogue: "Hello, Aunt Alicia."

The soldiers, becoming increasingly more anti-social, are wrangling zombie specimens in the caves around the bunker. Some are bitten, including Miguel, who's unjustly blamed for the attack, and the survivors quickly find themselves at odds with one another. Logan's been feeding parts of the dead soldiers to Bub, Sarah's been sleeping with Miguel—where's Miguel?—oh, that's right—he's outside, where, in an act of either revenge or delirium, he's allowed a horde of zombies into the complex of tunnels. The mayhem that ensues, the pursuit of the remaining survivors through the caves—don't go spelunking when there's zombies about!—

and Logan's lab scenes paradoxically wound up halving Romero's budget. George was told that he'd get the 7 million he wanted for *Day of the Dead* if he could wrangle an R-rating—he wouldn't, and the final $3.5 million version was unrated due to its bloody carnage.

The relationship between Logan and Bub is stunning, and the parallels to *Frankenstein* in the film run well beyond a simple nickname. Bub is played with pathos and pain by Sherman Howard, a TV regular who Romero considered to be the finest actor ever to wear a ghoul's makeup. Bub's trying to learn, trying to communicate, trying to figure out what he used to be—and what he's become—and when Bub confronts the cowardly and demonic Rhodes, we root for the big lug. He still lumbers, but ol' Bub has learned how to fire a gun.

Romero is introducing some concepts that he and other filmmakers would play on to varying degrees as the genre progressed from 1985 onward: zombies can learn, zombies might even be—domesticated? We can co-exist with the buggers? As in all Romero's pieces, the riffs on society's ills continue unabated; one gets the sense that Romero might have been more than a little perturbed by the gung-ho militarism of the Reagan era—heck, those mindless (commies? zombies?) turned out to be a bit more like us than we first imagined.

Music cues and dialogue about shopping malls refer back to *Dawn of the Dead*, but the film doesn't have any of the odd transitions that flawed *Dawn* slightly in the editing room. The bunker action was shot in a limestone mine outside Pittsburgh, and the zombie extras—including a Pop Warner football player and an undead clown—each were paid with single dollar. (They also picked up a copy of the paper used in the opening sequence and a cap that read "I played a zombie in *Day of the Dead*".) Although the movie's gained a cult following over the years (makeup maestro Tom Savini really pulls all the stops—and intestines—in this FX masterpiece), the strange, almost fairy-tale ending seems a bit of a letdown.

Day of the Dead Quiz
Answers on page 165.

Rating: DefCon 1
1. What do you see during George Romero's credit?

Rating: DefCon 2
2. What is the newspaper headline read during the opening credits?

Rating: DefCon 3
3. What is the book Bub is given?

Return of the Living Dead (1985)

The 1985 production of *Return of the Living Dead* is a B-movie down to its core—nearly every actor triggers a 'Hey! That's that guy who was in that one thing!' response.

It's a directorial debut, too, for one Dan O'Bannon, the gent who helped pen the breakthrough sci-fi/horror classic *Alien*. O'Bannon's hilariously dated *Return* had all the elements necessary for a cult classic: goofball leads, a decent dose of gross, and a little gratuitous nudity. Add a mid-80s punk rock soundtrack (available on record and cassette!), and voila—instant DVD must-have for geeks of a certain age.

The film opens at the Uneeda medical supply company where Frank (James Karen—that guy! From that one thing!) is showing off the med-school-bound cadavers to his newest assistant, Freddy. There are spares downstairs, too—drums of the dead who were the result of a horrible experiment from Pittsburgh in the '60s. Frank explains to his newbie that Romero's classic black-and-white zombie flick was based on actual events—and the evidence was mistakenly sent to Louisville, home of Uneeda. Alas, one tank springs a leak, and the gas inside has some pretty interesting side effects: it makes the living sick and reanimates another corpse in the freezer.

After a chemically-induced nap, Frank and Fred realize they've got a problem—a cadaver that won't stay dead. They call the boss, Burt (Clu Gulager—that other guy from that other thing!) and shortly discover that a shot to the brain was something that only worked in Romero's pictures. The solution? Cut the guy up and burn him with the help of mortician Ernie (Don Calfa—that bug-eyed pasty guy from that other *other* thing!). The ensuing smoke is released into a rain cloud, the rain falls on the local cemetery, and before long, Louisville is doomed.

As luck would have it, Freddy's punk-rock pals are hanging around the cemetery waiting for Fred's shift to wrap up. As zombies turn up in large numbers, they retreat indoors, where they encounter the cadaver from one of the tanks, now covered with a goop that inspires one delinquent to dub him 'Tarman'.

Tarman can express himself—he wants brains. For dinner. Right now. Frank and Freddy are soon dead themselves, EMT's and cops become food for the ghouls, and our survivors huddle in smaller and smaller groups as the military brings the nuclear option—with unforeseen, catastrophic results that set up the film's sequels nicely.

Return of the Living Dead is campy and comic, gory and gleeful—the actors clearly enjoyed every second of this bizarre zombie party. Mortician Ernie has a fondness for German martial music, military men are portrayed with gung-ho rigidity, and the notion of what constituted a 'punk' in the mind of a Hollywood producer in 1985 is as laughably, stereotypically off-base as Disney's portrayal of 1960's San Francisco hippies in *Herbie the Love Bug*. O'Bannon's zombies, unlike Romero's, have a little more spring in their step and display excellent communication skills—one tells our band of zombie-battlers that being dead is painful, it turns out, and eating brains eases the condition a bit.

Dan O'Bannon—who learned his chops by commiserating with John Carpenter—made it a rule that he wouldn't ever ask his actors to do anything he found impossible, and he himself munched on the calf's brains he'd brought in to sub for human ones. O'Bannon appeared in the film as a homeless gent and as a disembodied voice issuing commands from the authorities, and saved even more cash with some ingenious special effects: one scene features trash bags ostensibly containing quivering human limbs, but the bags are actually full of cymbal-banging monkey toys (sans cymbals, natch). Although the creators tried to get George Romero to produce the flick, Romero apparently didn't return their calls—but O'Bannon and company heard from some studio execs who tried to legally stop *Return* from using the phrase 'living dead' in the title. (The injunction failed.)

Return not only spawned sequel upon sequel, but cultivated a fan base as hungry for minutiae regarding the movies as Tarman is for brains. One fan named Michael Allred singlehandedly led the campaign for the film to be released on DVD, and there's an entire tome dedicated to the *Return* franchise alone written and archived by two gents obsessed with the rise and fall of the series. (The film's ever growing cult status has taken it beyond minor hit—it's made quite a bit more than the $4 million spent on production.) One of the funnier tributes in the film comes in the form of the African-American zombie hunter 'Spider'—he's got a Jheri-curl and costume that's very reminiscent of Michael Jackson in his *Thriller* days.

Return of the Living Dead Quiz
Answers on page 165.

Rating: DefCon 1

1. Which sequel came first: *Return of the Living Dead: Necropolis* or *Return of the Living Dead: Rave from the Grave*?

Rating: DefCon 2

2. The film is set in Kentucky, but it was actually shot where?

Rating: DefCon 3

3. Makeup and special effects designer Tony Gardner recently helped create the amputation scene for what 2010 Danny Boyle film?

Evil Dead II (1987)

Pity poor Bruce Campbell. He just can't take a vacation in peace—especially when he's playing 'Ash' in a Sam Raimi flick. He's even got to haul himself around in Sam's trademark ramshackle Oldsmobile.

Evil Dead II isn't a re-make of Raimi's first *Evil Dead* picture with a fatter budget, it's actually more of a sequel/continuation. Since Raimi couldn't obtain the rights to his first flick for a recap of what his primary character had undergone, he constructed about 15 minutes of new exposition at the beginning of the sequel: Ash and girlfriend crash at The Worst Cabin In America, Ash finds a tape deck and a book—and the dead start walking.

Ash has stumbled onto the medieval *Book of the Dead* and a spool of taped translations from the professor who owns the cabin. The recitations make the woods come alive, and a dark force steals away with Ash's main squeeze Linda (Denise Bixler). Linda returns as a zombie-fied 'Deadite', an evil incarnation that wants to do Ash in. Ash responds by decapitating her with a shovel—which, as is often the case in Raimi pictures, not terribly effective—so our hero dispatches his ex with a chainsaw.

As Ash battles the strange forces from the forest, his right hand becomes possessed—possessed to the point where the darn thing wants to cause Ash some serious harm. What ensues is the most gleefully awful 'Why-are-you-hitting-yourself?' Stooges-inspired series of sight gags that result with Ash separating himself from his willful appendage with a blood-splattered scream. Ash then tries to trap his own independently mobile severed hand under a bucket laden with books—including a copy of 'A Farewell to Arms'. Laughing yet? No? You will be.

While Ash battles the forces of evil in the woods, the professor's daughter and her boyfriend are making their way toward the cabin. The bridge is out—the bridge is always out in an *Evil Dead* movie—so to make it on foot to the cabin, Annie (Sarah Berry) enlists the help of a hillbilly local named Jake (Dan Hicks) and his gal Bobbie Joe (Kassie Wesley, playing a role inspired by Holly Hunter—one of Raimi's roommates when he was a starving filmmaker, along with Frances MacDormand and Joel Coen. Raimi had wanted Hunter for the role herself, but the producers opted for someone they felt had more sex appeal.).

Naturally, the group finds the cabin, naturally, the trail to the place disappears, and naturally, our group starts dropping like flies. Annie's mom Henrietta (played by Raimi's brother Ted in a monstrous latex suit) comes back to life, Annie's boyfriend becomes a Deadite, Bobby Joe is abused by the forest itself, even Ash becomes briefly possessed before Annie can save the day with a recitation of the spell which opens a portal—a portal that drags Ash through time to a truly inventive ending that wraps the story in upon itself.

A lot of critics and fans recognized *Evil Dead II* for what it really was—slapstick drenched in blood. Ash's disembodies hand scampers like a mouse, eyeballs pop out of heads and into mouths, but each and every sight gag is beautifully choreographed in the best Larry, Moe and Curly tradition. A few verbal gags make the cut here, too: one scene envisions Ash trying to calm himself in a mirror by telling himself he's fine. His reflection takes on a life of its own, uttering the response: "We just cut up our girlfriend with a chainsaw. Does that sound 'fine'?"

Even when Ash replaces his severed hand with a chainsaw, even when 'Posessed Henrietta' becomes a snake-like Deadite, *Evil Dead II* never seems to cross the line into ridiculousness—it manages to maintain a maniacal spirit of gory physical comedy without ever sliding into self-parody. It's also packed with references to other films, most notably *A Nightmare on Elm Street*. Wes Craven had paid tribute to Raimi with a number of nods to Sam's first *Evil Dead* film in his first Freddy Kreuger vehicle.

Another fan of Raimi's work was Stephen King: the film was financed by Dino DeLaurentis after King convinced DeLaurentis to put up the money (DeLaurentis had been working with King on the killer-truck laugher *Maximum Overdrive*.) Filmed for $3.6 million, the interiors were shot in a junior-high-school gym in North Carolina, the exteriors in the same Appalachian hills as the first.

Evil Dead II Quiz

Answers on page 165.

Rating: DefCon 1

1. Sam Raimi went on to direct three films in what Marvel Comics superhero franchise?

Rating: DefCon 2

2. Actor Bruce Campbell has what nickname based on a physical feature?

Rating: DefCon 3

3. What's the year, make and model of the car that's a trademark vehicle in Sam Raimi's films?

Truth in Advertising?

Rating: DefCon 3

Match the poster slogan to the movie it tried to sell. Answers on page 165.

Movie Titles

A. *Children Shouldn't Play With Dead Things* _____

B. *Dawn of the Dead* _____

C. *Day of the Dead* _____

D. *Dead and Buried* _____

E. *Sugar Hill* _____

F. *The Dead Pit* _____

G. *The Man They Could Not Hang* _____

H. *Zombie Nightmare* _____

I. *Zombies of Mora Tau* _____

Slogans

1. A Tide of Terror Floods the Screen.
2. It Will Take Your Breath Away . . . All of It.
3. Karloff Dares You to See This Holocaust of Horror!
4. The Darkest Day of Horror The World Has Ever Known!
5. The Mafia Has Never Met Anything Like Them!
6. When the Dead Start Walking, You'd Better Start Running . . .
7. When There's No More Room in Hell The Dead Will Walk the Earth.
8. You're Invited to Orville's "Coming-Party." it'll Be a Scream . . . Yours!
9. Your Worst Dreams are About to Come True!

Solution on page 171.

Across

1. Robe for a zombie in Old Rome
5. Asian nurse
9. Home of the Abominable Snowman
14. Greek god of love
15. Agatha Christie's *Death on the* ___
16. Make joyful
17. Walk like a zombie
18. Passed with flying colors
19. Liability's opposite
20. Encore of monster blood and guts (3 wds.)
23. French bread?
24. Flow's partner
25. Network that originally aired *The Outer Limits*
28. Old Toyota
30. Good-looker
32. Swiss peak in horror flick *Humains* (2009)
33. Obscene, like *Zombie Strippers*
37. *Blacula*-era hairstyle
38. See 33-Across
40. *Zombie Cheerleading Camp* cheer
41. Vocal tone after throat is torn by a zombie
42. June 6, 1944
43. Imaginary, like vampires?
46. "___ show time!"
47. Way out of a movie theatre
49. Rips apart
51. Color of Michael Jackson's jacket in *Thriller*
52. Ninny's brain size
54. *I'll Sleep When I'm Dead* (2004) star, Clive ___
55. Get stuffed on caviar (3 wds.)
60. Ration out
63. Lab gel
64. Condition of valuable horror movie toys, usually
65. Intended
66. Lousy reviews of horrible horror flicks
67. Brain wave
68. Amorous frog-frightening sow, Miss ___
69. Work in the cutting room on *Zombie Town*
70. Start for pool or pit

Down

1. School session
2. Black-and-white cookie
3. Zombie movie attendee
4. Dangerous condition on Freddy Krueger flick
5. What 20- or 55-Across is for GEORGE ROMERO
6. Film introduction?
7. On the safe side, at sea
8. Row of bushes to hide behind
9. Just around the corner
10. Ultimatum ender
11. Mas' mates
12. Had some eyeball soup
13. Allow
21. Yours and mine
22. What old-school zombies do to voodoo masters
25. Extramarital fling
26. Breaks out suddenly, as an alien from John Herd's ribcage
27. Hoofbeat sounds with the Headless Horseman
28. Potentially effective anti-zombie weapon: ___ hammer
29. Onward partner
31. Trophy for a matador
32. Tree sacred to the Druids
34. Ashes holder that breaks at the beginning of *Children of the Corn V*
35. Black gunk

36. ___ *Stink of Flesh*
39. Homophone of "die"
43. Cyberspace denizen
44. If everything goes wrong in a zombie attack (2 wds.)
45. Sinister look
48. Inconsistent
50. Lacking vitality, like a vampire's victim
53. Visibly shocked by a zombie
54. Muscat native

55. Sound that summoned Lurch on *The Addams Family*
56. 2010 Cannes Film Festival hit: ___, *Zombies!*
57. Wintry horror flick: *Slay* ___ (2009)
58. Snake eyes
59. Flight data, briefly
60. Rock concert equipment
61. Oahu Zombie Walk garland
62. Time delay

The Serpent and the Rainbow (1988)

Four years after giving America yet another cause for sleep deprivation with *A Nightmare on Elm Street*, Wes Craven went to Haiti with a script adapted from a non-fiction book under his arm. That book was a best-selling chronicle of anthropologist Wade Davis's trip to the island nation to investigate the drug-induced zombie-fication of human beings steeped in voodoo religious practices. Davis had sold his work, which bore the same name as the film, expecting that Peter Weir would direct and Mel Gibson would star in the picture. The star and director were changed, but the basic concept—that zombie behavioral tendencies could be readily explained with the right powder in a petri dish—survived. Bill Pullman plays Dennis Alan, an academe who's researching the case of a gent who was dead, buried, and then spotted around town in a much livelier state. Alan and his corporate backers are convinced that the same dope that makes zombies could be modified to create a powerful, even life-saving anesthetic. Alan's been all over the world ingesting psychedelics in the name of science—in fact, if Dennis Hopper had ever shot a zombie flick, this is probably what it would've played like. (Think Indiana Jones in *Altered States*.)

Dennis falls in with a local doctor, Marielle Duchamp (Cathy Tyson), and begins investigating the local culture and rituals. He's helped by a nightclub owner named Lucien (Paul Winfield) and con artist/voodoo shaman named Louis Mozart (Brent Jennings). Mozart knows the formula and the religious practices needed to create the powder that, when even applied to the skin, induces a death-like trance. The rub? Voodoo is a powerful tool for the local enforcers in the second Duvalier administration; in fact, the head of the neighborhood secret police, the *Tonton Macoute*, Captain Dargent Peytraud (played with evil aplomb by Zakes Moake), steals the souls of the undead and keeps them in jars.

Captain Peytraud is also pretty fond of torture—knowing what Dr. Alan's up to, the good Captain arrests Dennis, straps him to a specially-made wooden chair and drives a nail through—um, *the worst possible place*. Dennis remains undeterred, and embarks on a three-day-long process to distill the zombie drug with Mozart and Dr. Duchamp. Before the process wraps, Peytraud frames Alan for the death of a young girl; waking from a nightmare in a beach house, Alan is horrified to learn his bed-mate is a decapitated corpse. Dennis is forced to leave Haiti—his return would mean a murder trial—but Mozart helps him smuggle the powder back to the states.

Back home in Boston, Doctor Alan realizes pretty quickly that Captain Peytraud is a master of the dark arts—he can possess anybody, even the wife of the CEO that's commissioned his work. Additionally, Dennis cannot reach Marielle, with whom he's become quite smitten. Dennis returns to Haiti for a final tangle with the evil Peytraud, a battle that will see Doctor Alan himself become, briefly, a victim of the Captain's nefarious talents.

Craven departed from the zombie fare American audiences were accustomed to—the undead look a little pasty, but they're nothing like the rotting cannibals that Romero brought to the screen 20 years earlier. They're slaves to their master Peytraud, a *bokor* of the worst order, and they're well aware that they're being controlled by the evil black magician. The thugs of the *Tonton Macoute* are the bad guys here; the zombies are completely sympathetic figures. The film is loaded with Craven's beloved nightmare sequences, in fact, it's suggested that zombies and their masters can enter people's dreams (sound familiar?).

More thriller than horror show, *Serpent* plays against two backdrops— the desperately poor, breathtakingly beautiful Haiti and the brutality and eventual collapse of the regime of Jean-Claude 'Baby Doc' Duvalier. The movie was shot on location in Haiti until life began to imitate art—political unrest forced Craven's production over to the Dominican Republic halfway through shooting. Bill Pullman—who found a nice haircut and stuck with it for his whole career—played alongside a variety of extremely dangerous animals including a jaguar and poisonous spiders and snakes, and Pullman's wife pops up as an extra, a blonde tourist dabbling in a bit of voodoo herself.

The Serpent and the Rainbow Quiz
Answers on page 165.

Rating: DefCon 1
1. Bill Pullman saved the world as a U.S. President in what film?

Rating: DefCon 2
2. The ad line for *The Serpent and the Rainbow* stated "Don't bury me . . . I'm ___ ___."

Rating: DefCon 3
3. Director Wes Craven, whose other films include *The Last House on the Left*, *The Hills Have Eyes*, *The People Under the Stairs*, and *Scream* did a 180 in 1999 by directing *Music of the Heart* featuring what acclaimed actress as a violinist teaching in East Harlem?

Dead Alive (Braindead) (1992)

Pity poor Lionel Cosgrove. He's a klutz, his dad's dead, his domineering, mother doesn't like his Latina girlfriend—and now Mum's a zombie to boot. Peter Jackson—yes, the same Peter Jackson behind the incredibly successful *Lord of the Rings* film trilogy—was the mad scientist responsible for the gag-fest called *Dead Alive* (known as *Braindead* in Jackson's native New Zealand), widely regarded as the goriest film ever made.

It's 1957 in beautiful New Zealand, and Lionel is trying pitch woo to the lovely shopkeeper Paquita. During a trip to the zoo, the couple's followed by the overbearing Vera—Lionel's mum—who winds up being bitten by a monkey. The bite from this critter is lethal . . . well, kind of. Parts start dropping off of mother, and before you know it, Vera's a re-animated corpse whose first meal is her own nurse. Zombie Vera is ultimately run over by a local tram as she tries to follow Lionel to Paquita's family business, and Vera winds up buried—temporarily.

Lionel tries to arrest the zombie plague by keeping Vera and her first few victims under wraps—turns out a dose of animal tranquilizer keeps these zombies pretty docile. Lionel's uncle Les, however, believing Lionel to be some kind of psycho-sexual killer who keeps bodies in the cellar, blackmails the young lad (Les wants the family riches) and celebrates by throwing a party in the stately home Vera has bequeathed to Lionel.

Paquita discovers the zombies downstairs in Lionel's house, and Lionel explains his issues—even though Mother's a re-animated corpse, he can't bring himself to finish her off. Paquita convinces poor Lionel to give the zombies a dose of poison with the same needle he's been using to sedate 'em. Trouble is, that chemical's only poisonous when ingested by humans. It's an animal stimulant that seems to give zombies even more strength than they'd have ordinarily.

The party rapidly devolves into a zombie dinner-dance, and soon Lionel's forced to mow down the undead by the dozen—literally. Lionel raises the business end of the grass-cutter he uses on the lawn, and the resulting carnage is impossible to justly describe with mere words. Mix in a backstory where Mum turns out to be guilty of some pretty horrible crimes, add a reborn Vera who's grown three times her original size, and you've got a climax that would give a Hobbit second thoughts about ever working with Jackson again.

Dead Alive takes every possible zombie convention and expands it to its logical—and bloody—extreme, then adds a few new wrinkles to the rules of zombie existence. There's zombie lust betwixt the nurse and an undead Reverend (who meets his initial end fighting zombies with his martial arts moves). There's a zombie baby whom Lionel pushes through the park in a pram, only to have the little bugger escape and force Lionel to issue some pretty extreme corporal punishment. There's a head in a blender, there's a greaser zombie in a toilet, there's not one but *two* grisly scenes around the Cosgrove family dining table that really push the limits of what any but the most iron-stomached viewers can reasonably . . . digest?

Zombie parts in *Dead Alive* don't know the meaning of the word 'quit'. Torsos, arms, legs, even internal organs keep after their living victims. The old notion of a blow to the head doesn't seem to have too much effect on these drooling ghouls—their only enemy seems to be fire. Unless, that is, you manage to liquefy what's left, and *Dead Alive* includes quite a bit of liqui-fication. Additionally, the zombies here are hungry for humans, sure, but darn near anything will do—Paquita has cause to issue the line, "Your mother ate my dog!", which became the title for the film's Spanish release.

There's some debate about the claim that *Dead Alive* is the goriest film ever—there are reports the amount of movie blood used here tops anything ever shot (the lawnmower-zombie-massacre reportedly used five gallons *per second*)—but there's no argument that the film was heavily cut for release in some countries. The unrated DVD available in the US isn't even complete—a few scenes never made it out of NZ. The movie's splatter-factor is tempered with a Bugs Bunny-meets-Monty Python slapstick sensibility: there are scenes that play like a bloody cartoon. Jackson brought the picture in under budget, only to see the name changed for its stateside release so audiences wouldn't confuse it with Roger Corman's 1990 film *Brain Dead*.

Dead Alive (Braindead) Quiz

Answers on page 165.

Rating: DefCon 1

1. The film opens on what island—a reference to 1933's *King Kong*, which Jackson would reboot over a decade after *Dead Alive* was released?

Rating: DefCon 2

2. In the fight in the park, zombie baby gets hit in the head with what piece of playground equipment?

Rating: DefCon 3

3. What sort of monkey bites Vera?

Cemetery Man (1994)

Arty and odd, sexy and weirdly comic, *Cemetery Man* is based on a novel by Tiziano Sclavi, who's best known in his home country of Italy as the pen behind a horror comic called *Dylan Dog*. *Dylan Dog*'s protagonist looks a bit like Rupert Everett—which undoubtedly helped Everett get the gig. This import—known in its home country as *Dellamorte Dellamore* (*Of Death, Of Love*)—was shot a few years before Everett gained fame in the US as a Julia Roberts film-squeeze.

Everett, in the role of Francesco Dellamorte, plays a gravekeeper whose primary duties include tending to the digs with the assistance of his lumpy, halfwitted assistant Gnaghi—and plugging zombies in the head with his pistol. The dead—for reasons entirely left unexplained—have a tendency to pop up and gnaw on the living seven days after they pass. Francesco seems grimly content to play the part of the local weirdo—there's a rumor in town that he's impotent, and the village motorcycle punks remind poor Dellamorte of this every time he drives his VW bug into the town of Buffalora to get paid.

The rumor's quickly proven untrue, as a woman comes by the cemetery to bury her husband. Although the crypt-keeper mistakes the dead gent for the girl's father, she explains to Francesco that the old coot was her greatest lover—that is, until Francesco discovers that the old boneyard makes the young lady feel very, very amorous. The girl, credited only as 'She', is played by Finnish-born actress Anna Falchi, who was clearly cast for her startling augmentations. (Not that this is a bad thing, mind you. If we may offer an editorial remark here, let's just go with 'Wow'.)

The young lass's hookup with Francesco on top of her late hubby's grave (they shared everything) infuriates the dead guy, who crawls out of the dirt to gnaw on his widow. Thinking the bite's killed his love, Francesco fires a bullet at the girl, a glancing blow to the noggin that drops his re-animated BFF—for a while. Mix in a motorcycle-gang versus bus-full-of-boy-scouts disaster, and pretty soon the Buffalora graveyard is quite the happening place after sunset. 'She' climbs out of her tomb—Francesco had actually killed her while she was still alive—and their attempt at re-union is interrupted by Gnaghi as the lady tries to make dinner out of Francesco.

If the plot seems a bit weird to this point, well, you've only just gotten a taste of the lunacy that develops in the film's final 30 minutes. 'She' seems to come back into Francesco's life a la Kim Novak in *Vertigo*, but with more alarming regularity. (Anna Falchi had actually played Kim Novak in another Italian flick the same year that *Cemetery Man* was produced.) 'She' is the new mayor's assistant with a phobia of manhood that Francesco tries to address with a trip to the local surgeon (don't ask) and later, 'She' turns out to be a hooker as well.

Gnaghi, meanwhile, has fallen in love with a disembodied head, and the sum total of everything Francesco's seen and done starts to drive him nutty enough to start whacking the living with his gun. Death has told Dellamorte to stop shooting his minions—if you want to rob Death of the whole reanimation bit, shoot those who aren't dead in the skull. As the plot continues to twist into more and more bizarre realms, it seems as if director Michele Soavi might be setting us up for an 'all-a-bad-dream-in-the-mind-of-a-madman' finish. Not so fast, dear zombie fan, not so fast.

Cemetery Man is loaded with sight gags—the portrait on the late hubby's gravestone changes, seemingly reacting to events, Francesco seems to be on the phone every time zombies come knockin', and a young girl's talking head winds up subbing for a TV picture tube. The visual references don't stop with puns—a shrouded kiss is lifted directly from a surrealist painting by Renee Magritte called 'The Lovers' and there's a motorcycle that charges out of the grave in what must be a nod to the cover art featured on a popular '80s album cover (see quiz, below). Everett plays Dellamorte with about as much detachment as he could muster while slaughtering both the living and the ghouls, but his trysts with Falchi literally raise the dead and set the bed on fire.

Cemetery Man would be beautiful to look at even without Anna Falchi—the location shots in Guardea, Italy make a stunning backdrop to the grim goings-on in the cemetery. Workers had to clear some bones out of an actual crypt for one shot, and they hurriedly returned the human remains to their proper place the next day after one crew member said he'd been visited by a ghost.

Cemetery Man Quiz
Answers on page 165.

Rating: DefCon 1

1. What album is paid homage to in the *Cemetery Man* sequence where a motorcycle emerges from a grave?

Rating: DefCon 2

2. Rupert Everett has played a number of not-quite-human characters since *Cemetery Man*. Name the film in which he played:
   a. A fairy king named Oberon
   b. An animated Prince Charming
   c. A fox
   d. The villainous "Dr. Claw"

Rating: DefCon 3

3. What famed mainstream film director said that *Cemetery Man* was one of the bet films to come out of Italy in the 1990s?

Musical Interlude: The Zombies

When The Zombies were signed to Decca Records, the name conjured up images more creepy than gory, and the cover shot for the debut album is only as horrifying as the average high school graduation picture. Ironically, the promo material for the band focused on brains—not for food, but for thought. "Are they Britain's Brainiest Beat Group?" ponders a subtitle as the fellas review their secondary education marks in an early set of photos promoting the combo.

Formed in 1961, The Zombies knocked around St. Albans, England for three years until they entered the 'Herts Beat' competition, sponsored by the *London Evening News*. Keyboardist and songwriter Rod Argent knew that the band would begin to drift apart before long, and Decca had promised a record deal to the winner. The Zombies won—but Decca was so taken with the lads that the band had already been offered a contract during the semi-final round. The band's first release in the UK, 'Begin Here', included—among the R&B covers typical for bands of the era—a shimmering lush-pop gem entitled 'She's Not There' (penned solely by Argent with plaintive vocals from Colin Blunstone) which crossed the pond and became a hit in the States.

A US release followed (simply titled 'The Zombies'), which lifted some tracks from the British disc and added a few others. Still, it was the jazz-and-classical-informed style of 'She's Not There' that drove the band's early popularity on both sides of the Atlantic. Argent, along with the band's other songwriter, bassist Chris White, was helping invent progressive rock (also called art rock or prog rock) a genre which would be taken to its most luscious—and often ridiculous—extremes by bands like The Moody Blues, King Crimson, Yes, and Emerson, Lake and Palmer. At first, however, many of their contemporaries lifted some of The Zombies' vocal harmonies and major-minor key shifts.

The band began touring the US, starting in the American south for Dick Clark on a bill that included Motown girl-group The Velvettes. Members of The Zombies walked into a diner with the ladies—arms around one another—and the sight of a gaggle of longhaired Caucasians embracing a trio of black ladies was apparently a bit too much for the locals. Argent told an interviewer from retrosellers.com that, " . . . the manager shepherded all of us out . . . he said, 'We're lucky you didn't get shot'." Soon The Zombies were playing Murray the K's NYC Christmas shows (where drummer Hugh Grundy was pressed into service revving the motorcycle engine for the Shangri-La's performance of their hit 'Leader of the Pack').

In 1967, The Zombies signed with CBS and recorded 'Odessey and Oracle' ('Odessey' was misspelled by the cover artist), but the group was already weary of the business—they'd been unable to reproduce the success of 'She's Not There', and that, coupled with the pressures of touring, split the band up before 'Odessey and Oracle' was even released. After foundering for a year, Al Kooper (another CBS artist) heard the disc and began a campaign to get his label to get behind the recording, and the single 'Time of the Season' began to get airplay in the States, eventually hitting #3 on the Billboard charts.

'Odessey' has been ranked at #80 by Rolling Stone's '500 Greatest Albums of All Time' survey of critics and musicians. Among the disc's notable features is the early use of a mellotron to stand in for strings and horns—the actual instruments weren't in the budget for a band with such limited commercial output.

After the breakup, the band refused to tour to support the success of 'Odessey' in America, but some faux-Zombies groups began to cash in, performing under the name without a single original member in the lineup. Rod Argent was already involved in his own band, Argent, by this time, eventually releasing the classic rock staple 'Hold Your Head Up' in 1972. Chris Blunstone did some solo vocal work—including a few tracks for the Alan Parsons Project—before re-uniting with Argent at the beginning of the 21st century to put The Zombies back on bills for patrons waxing nostalgic for the British Invasion.

28 Days Later (2002)

George Romero never won an Oscar for Best Director. Neither did Alfred Hitchcock, Robert Altman, or Stanley Kurbrick.

On the other hand, Frank Capra, Sydney Pollack, Clint Eastwood and just about every other Academy Award winner for Best Director never made a zombie film.

But Danny Boyle did both, winning an Oscar for *Slumdog Millionaire* just six years after helping reignite the zombie genre with *28 Days Later*.

From the beginning, this doesn't feel like the zombie films that came before it. The flick opens with animal rights activists (perhaps part of the crew from *12 Monkeys*) unwisely breaking into a testing lab. There they are warned about "the Rage," an infection that is causing the monkeys to behave not-so-adorably.

Of course, this would be a short instead of a feature if the do-gooders *didn't* open a cage and let out a raging chimp.

Flash forward—guess how many days?— and a British bike messenger wakes up alone in a hospital. Well, not exactly alone. Rage-infected zombies . . . fast zombies . . . soon give chase. Survivors are discovered. Survivors are infected. Tough life-or-death decisions must be made.

The group of survivors eventually finds its way to a mansion where there's a very human problem. The guy in charge—who thinks the solution is to wait until the zombies starve to death for lack of people to eat—is a nutcase who thinks that the population has to be rebuilt whether the available women like it or not. Thereafter, the fighting is as much mano-a-mano as mano-a-zombie.

Oh, and maybe, just maybe, there isn't a world-wide epidemic. Maybe, just maybe, England has been quarantined.

Boyle managed to save a bundle on sets by using London itself—for example, he was granted a complete shutdown of the city's streets for an hour daily, and in order to inform drivers they'd have to take an alternate route, Boyle enlisted attractive young women to make the pronouncements to motorists. (It worked—there were very few reports of rage spawned by road.) The irony here? It was the very societal aspect of the-always-angry worker drone that inspired the notion of the rage virus itself.

Screenwriter Alex Garland, working with Boyle, determined that we all get the fictional mutants right for our times depending on where we happen to be on the cultural arc. Fear of the effects of radiation was the impetus for previous generation's zombie parties, but Garland and Boyle tapped into the notion that a viral infection that turned regular folks homicidal was just what we'd all fear the most at the turn of the new century. After the horrors of 9/11 and the emergence of new diseases worldwide, the pair felt like they'd touched upon our newest common nightmares.

They were right—the film was, and is, a monster hit (pardon the pun). Since its original release, *28 Days Later* has made over six times its original $8 million budget. And even though we include it here, Garland and Boyle remain absolutely adamant that *28 Days Later* is most assuredly not a zombie movie. It's a flick about disease and mutation, not the living dead. Despite their opinions about the film, the posters for the US release included lines like: 'Danny Boyle reinvents the zombie horror film . . . '

Like Romero before him, Boyle did actually re-invent the zombie movie. Everything was fair game; especially the rage virus's curious effect on its victims—they act like zombies, but with a terrific ability to sprint. (Actual athletes were cast as the ghouls, in fact.) The look of the film was as revolutionary as Romero's, too: digital video in 2002 had a harsh and unrelenting look which made it as evening-news-effective as the hand-held black-and-white camera work found in *Night of the Living Dead* in 1968. In the same way that Romero infused his pictures with social commentary, Boyle researched civil unrest, viral infections, countries that had devolved into anarchy—anything he could to make the experience that much more gripping. Despite a broad range of possible endings that had been kicked around for the picture, Boyle still decided to end the film on a positive note—maybe the whole world hadn't gone to hell, after all.

Like previous successful zombie films, Danny Boyle cast mostly unknowns throughout, including Cilan Murphy, Naomie Harris and Brendan Gleeson. As complete as the film may have been, the success of *28 Days Later* led to the expected sequel, *28 Weeks Later*. This time, Boyle turned over the directing reigns to Juan Carlos Fresnadillo, instead serving as a co-producer.

28 Days Later Quiz

Answers on page 166.

Rating: DefCon 1

1. What brand of soda does our hero find in the abandoned hospital?

Rating: DefCon 2

2. How does Frank get infected?

Rating: DefCon 3

3. On the road, a sign reads "Last cheeseburgers for _____ miles".

Resident Evil (2002)

Before *Resident Evil* was a film, it had already been a wildly successful video game series that was first introduced for the Sony Playstation in 1996. The game was the brainchild of Shinji Mikami, a Japanese developer who'd titled the game *Biohazard* for Capcom in his home country. The movie version had been originally scripted by George Romero, but the zombie-master's take on the game was ultimately rejected. As will sometimes happen in Hollywood, the project sat dormant until it was handed to Paul W.S. Anderson, who wrote and directed the flick for its 2002 release.

The great thing about video games? You've always got the tools you need to slaughter whatever critter turns up—and there's always a way out of the dead-end-hallway full of zombies. *Resident Evil* plays like a video game, its characters—well, 'characters' might be an overstatement, given some of the acting in this effort—worming their way through the levels of an underground 'hive': the headquarters of the profoundly nasty Umbrella Corporation. After something very, very wrong occurs in the hive, a team of commandos goes in, aided by a couple who can't seem to remember that they were busily guarding the top secret entrance to the hive, housed in a mansion above ground. (Nerve-gas-induced amnesia, you see. As one of the main characters utters later in the movie: 'It's a long story.')

The female half of our gatekeeping duo is Alice, played by Milla Jovovich in all her wooden, nightgown-and-combat-boot-clad hotness. As Alice's memory slowly returns, we learn that the big mean corporation had been working on something called the T virus, which, in addition to being stored in the most fragile little glass vials imaginable, will kill everyone fairly quickly and then re-animate them into lumbering undead ghouls with a predisposition for cannibalism. Someone was trying to steal both the virus and its antidote, and after a bit of the bug was released into the hive, the building's controlling supercomputer, dubbed the 'Red Queen', had closed up the joint and murdered everyone inside. (The film actually opens with the wanton destruction of all the hive's white collar paper pushers and lab techs in an illustration of what may be the worst round of corporate layoffs ever.)

The computer (creepily voiced by a little British girl) is trying to knock off the commando squad, the zombies are out to snack on anything retaining the ability to reason, mutant Dobermans want to nibble on Alice (and really, who doesn't?), and for the real kicker, there's also an early-experiment-gone-horribly-wrong roaming the hallways of the hive. He (she? it?) was a subject who'd had what must've been way too many shots of the T virus, and has mutated into something kind of similar to Jeff Goldblum in *The Fly*. Alice turns out to be a whistle-blowing employee of Umbrella, her sham husband Spence turns out to be a profiteer (think of a better-looking Wayne Knight in *Jurassic Park*), and Michelle Rodriguez in the role of commando 'Rain' delivers a performance lifted directly from the lady-Marine Private Vasquez in *Aliens*.

The film wraps where most zombie films begin: after waking in some kind of bizarre hospital theatre, Alice walks the streets of the empty and ruined above-ground Raccoon City, where we glimpse a shot of a newspaper headlined 'THE DEAD WALK!', the same headline seen at the start of Romero's *Day of the Dead*.

Yeah, this movie lifts everything. Most critics hated the thing, but audiences dug it. After grossing over $100 million worldwide, Alice returned for the inevitable sequels. The film is jammed with the kind of gaps in logic that make video games entertaining—if a computer has the ability to cut you up with a whole bunch of lasers, why start out sending just one at a time?—but that's part of the fun here. It's a classic action war picture, but the enemy is mainly an army of slow-witted corpses. If you've played the games and you want a bit more biohazard but don't have 100 minutes to spare on the flick, no problem—there's also *Resident Evil* comic books.

The soundtrack is loaded with metal, including the lovely ballad 'My Plague' by Slipknot. Execs from both the Japanese and American arms of Capcom appear as zombies in the film (wow, that's irony).

Resident Evil Quiz
Answers on page 166.

Rating: DefCon 1
 1. Which lesser movie in the *Alien* series did Anderson also direct?

Rating: DefCon 2
 2. What are the full titles of the three *Resident Evil* sequels?

Rating: DefCon 3
 3. Why was the film's original subtitle dumped?

Shaun of the Dead (2004)

Simon Pegg and Edgar Wright constructed the funniest British zombie movie ever—now that's a niche—with 2004's *Shaun of the Dead*, a priceless romp that's equal parts gags, gore, romance and melodrama. Shaun, played by co-writer Pegg, is a nametag-wearing, appliance-selling drone who finds himself on the outs with his girlfriend, her flatmates, his step-dad and one of the two gents he shares a flat with in London. The cause of his problems seems to be his best bud Ed (Nick Frost), a slovenly roommate who cusses, farts, drinks beer and plays video games, subsidizing his lifestyle by selling the odd bag of weed.

After being dumped by his gal Liz, Shaun ties one on with Ed at their favorite hangout, a pub called the Winchester. The ensuing hangover causes Shaun to be fairly indifferent to the behavior of his neighbors (not to mention the television news) the following morning—that is, until two zombies turn up in the yard. A battle using old LP's, a shovel, and a very British piece of sporting equipment ensues until Shaun hatches a plan to rescue his mom and his girlfriend and hole up in his ex's least favorite place, the Winchester. Borrowing the ride of their other now zombiefied roomie, Shaun and Ed run to Shaun's mum's, only to find stepdad Phillip (played by Bill Nighy, who's quite possibly appeared in every British comedy made in the last 15 years) has been bitten.

Phillip passes while the now fully assembled group, including Liz and her roommates David (a wimpy sort who's got a rush on Liz) and David's girlfriend and wanna-be actress Dianne, are driving toward the pub. Phil turns flesh-eater, forcing the crew to abandon Phil's Jag and hike to the Winchester on foot. After Shaun distracts a horde of the undead to allow his pals access to the pub, the group hunkers down—only to discover that Shaun's mom Barbra has been bitten. David insists that Barb needs to be shot—which leads to the funniest Mexican standoff ever shot using a gun, broken bottles and a corkscrew.

The ghouls access the pub after taking down David and Dianne—David is gutted in classic Romero style—and gnawing on Ed. Busting out of the Winchester's cellar, a re-united Shaun and Liz discover that the British Army is moving in, mowing down the critters by the dozens. The film's upbeat finish is at once sunny and nasty, two words which make for great descriptors of the movie as a whole. The script from Pegg and Wright,

directed by Wright, manages to bring as much gore and gristle as any serious zombie flick without compromising the comic romance between Shaun and Liz or the genuine friendship between Shaun and Ed. Whip-crack dialogue and editing worthy of both the best horror and comedy flicks of the 21st century complete the treat.

Pegg and Frost had starred in a UK TV series called *Spaced* that had been directed by Wright, and fans of the series were recruited to play zombie extras in *Shaun*—for which they were paid the princely sum of a single pound sterling. After wrapping shooting for an estimated 4 million pounds, the film's release was delayed for two weeks in the UK because *Shaun*'s initial release date fell on the same weekend that the re-boot of 2004's *Dawn of the Dead* debuted. While George Romero was disappointed with the frenetic video-game action of the remake of *Dawn*, Romero absolutely loved *Shaun* and recruited Pegg and Wright as extras in *Land of the Dead*. Romero was given a private screening at his home—and apparently missed a few references to his films; *Shaun* nods to both Romero's work and the British 'rage-virus' epic *28 Days Later*.

Pegg and Wright's final cut proved to be a worldwide hit, pulling in more than $30 million (USD) and finding itself ranked by viewers of BBC TV Channel 4 as the third best British comedy ever made. Critics loved the film as much as audiences, and the charm of the film can be summed up thusly: you'll hear the F-bomb 77 times, but you'll learn what the word 'exacerbate' means.

Shaun of the Dead Quiz
Answers on page 166.

Rating: DefCon 1
1. What piece of sports equipment does Shaun use for a weapon?

Rating: DefCon 2
2. As what did the date of the zombie invasion later become known?

Rating: DefCon 3
3. What one-royalty-word band performs the closing song in the film?

Dawn of the Dead (2004)

It's wrong to call Zack Snyder's 2004 *Dawn of the Dead* a remake of George Romero's classic of the same name. Like the original, it's got a) a bunch of survivors holing up in a mall, and b) more zombies than regular folks. But that's where the similarities end. Romero's name appears in the credits, but only as an inspiration—George believed the bulk of the movie felt more like a video game.

First and foremost—and this is a detail that Romero really didn't like—these zombies *run*. Taking a cue from the incredibly agile critters first introduced to fans of flesh eaters in *28 Days Later*, re-animation can turn even the fattest middle-aged granny into a track star. Seriously, one could make a case for a Zombie Olympics if these ghouls are the norm.

The opening minutes of the film are horrifying and heart wrenching; Ana, a nurse played by Sarah Polley, awakens to find her husband being attacked by a little girl who lives down the street. Hubby soon gets a hankerin' for more than a hickey from Ana, and in moments our heroine is driving through the Milwaukee suburbs that have become the setting for unbridled madness. (It's difficult not to wince during this sequence— especially in a post-9/11 world.) She meets a cop played by Ving Rhames, who does a tremendous job playing Ving Rhames, and soon the pair come across three other survivors who are headed for the local mall.

Like the original, the setting of a shopping emporium offers some pretty funny commentary: mall cops are self important jerks, and the ever-present muzak titles mirror the action in a pretty amusing way. ("You Light Up My Life" has never sounded more comic.) Unlike the original, the social messages in the mall scenes don't feel nearly as biting. (Pun intended.) The number of survivors grows with the arrival of a truckload of refugees—and that number is diminished by living and undead alike. The survivors make contact with a gun shop owner named Andy who's stranded on a rooftop across the street from the mall, and an attempt to help the loner results in one of the most frightening scenes in the film: a young girl threatened by the reanimated Andy broadcasts her plight via walkie-talkie. All the action in this scene is off camera—a lesson the director could have applied elsewhere.

Pregnant zombies, baby zombies, literally hundreds of different heads being blown off of running corpses—take out the brain or burn 'em, folks!—the special effects are excellent (the budget ran over $28 million), but ultimately the movie becomes an incredibly nihilistic action film as our merry band of mall walkers heads for the docks for a boat to get them out of town and onto an island in Lake Michigan. Don't punch out when the credits roll—there's action interspersed with the end titles that seems to suggest that the human race is pretty much sunk, at least in Wisconsin.

The soundtrack ranges from outstanding (Johnny Cash) to ham-handed cheeseball irony (a lounge version of Disturbed's "Down With the Sickness"? Really?) and about half the dialogue seems to include the phrase 'Let's go!', but the flick delivers what zombie fans really want: zombies mass, zombies bite, zombies lose their heads. Especially Andy.

The unrated DVD/Blu Ray director's cut contains about 12 extra minutes of gore and a great feature on how to blow up a human head without harming an actor. Oh, and boobies, too.

Dawn of the Dead Quiz
Answers on page 166.

Rating: DefCon 1

1. True or false; Characters in George Romero's *Dawn of the Dead* have the same names as characters in Zack Snyder's *Dawn of the Dead*.

Rating: DefCon 2

2. Which Canadian-born star of this film was independently wealthy for her TV work by age 14?

Rating: DefCon 3

3. One of the stores in the mall was named after a star in the original. Name it.

Land of the Dead (2005)

George Romero's fourth *Dead* installment imagines a city—Pittsburgh, sometime in the future, or perhaps maybe the mid-70s—that's divvied up into three distinct classes after the zombie apocalypse: the rich, lorded over by the corrupt Mr. Kaufman (Dennis Hopper), the working stiffs (foragers, soldiers, vendors, hookers) and the literal bottom feeders (flesh-eating zombies). Society at large has, of course, pretty much gone to pot with walking corpses roaming through every zip code.

The well-to-do live in a high-rise called 'Fiddler's Green' at the center of the spit of land at the confluence of the 'Burgh's three rivers while the lower caste lives in the slums surrounding the place. Cholo (John Leguizamo) and Riley (Simon Baker in his pre-TV *Mentalist* days) command bands of foragers who venture out into the small surrounding towns to scrounge canned goods—and whatever Cholo can sell on the black market, primarily liquor and cigars.

Cholo's upwardly mobile—Kaufman owes him cash, and Cholo wants an apartment in the Green. Mr. K dislikes Hispanics and the undead equally, so he denies Cholo his due, and Cholo responds by stealing an armored vehicle nicknamed 'Dead Reckoning' that carries enough ordinance to level the high-rise. Cholo wants his money by midnight, or the shelling will commence.

Kaufman recruits Riley, the builder of the zombie-killin' Humvee, to retrieve the vehicle. Riley, on the outs with Big K for saving a working girl from a competitive-eating cage match in which she was bait for a pair of extra-large zombies, is offered his freedom along with the aforementioned pro and his slow-witted crack-shot sidekick Charlie.

The monkeywrench here? Although they're still painfully slow—a Romero hallmark—the walking dead have gotten wise. They are, in fact, quicker to unionize than their human counterparts. Led by a zombie you can actually sympathize with, a massive former gas-station owner with the name 'Big Daddy' embroidered on his work shirt, the undead learn how to wield weapons, fire rifles, and—this is key—cross rivers. Realizing that the dead really have no use for oxygen, the zombies take a stroll across the riverbed of one of the city's two natural boundaries, feasting first on the oppressed worker-folk who huddle around the Green. (Once again, it's the middle class getting devoured from both sides.)

The undead have also learned not to be distracted by fireworks Riley and Cholo's crews launch when they'd rather have the critters—'stenches', as they've come to be known—looking elsewhere while they're either scrounging up whiskey or reloading.

Romero's 2005 *Land* proved that even with a fat budget by George's standards—16 million—Romero hadn't lost the knack for wry social commentary. Roger Ebert pointed out that the Green was reminiscent of retirement villages, its inhabitants 'condemned to leisure'. Happy shopping-mall-and-restaurant livin' is soon turned into a giant buffet for an army of self-educated zombies, and Riley sagely points out that the barricaded point of land will soon become a death-trap for everyone within. As in all of George's films, human nature is more despicable than zombie-nature; the undead only want dinner, but the living will murder for money, power, and material goods.

Ever frugal—and knowing he'd need to keep things from spinning into an NC-17 rating from the MPAA—Romero layered some scenes with obscuring elements in the theatrical release that he was able to strip away for the unrated director's cut on DVD. Both versions include plenty of zombie-noshin' and brain-splatterin' (NOTE: a zombie is not out of commission even if the head is still just *slightly* attached), but Romero really allows his characters to take shape in this outing—even the ones who can't really utter dialogue too well.

The final smack-down betwixt Hopper's contemptible Kaufman and a zombie-fied Cholo amps up the racism of the wealthy before K gets his comeuppance. Romero is just about at his grisly best with the gore here; heads are turned to ghoulash, tendons snap like rubber bands and a human arm is split like a chicken's wishbone in one inventive shot.

The film includes a zombie-cameo—Simon Pegg and Edgar Wright, two of the geniuses behind *Shaun of the Dead*—turn up in full makeup, chained in their scene so that the living can pose with the undead for souvenir photos in a seedy bar outside the Green. The pair also turn up on the cover of the commercial DVD.

Land of the Dead Quiz
Answers on page 166.

Rating: DefCon 1
1. What are "sky flowers"?

Rating: DefCon 2
2. *Land* is the first George Romero zombie film to cast recognizable stars in key roles. Who do we see first in the film, Dennis Hopper or John Leguizamo?

Rating: DefCon 3
3. In the opening sequence, what musical instrument is a zombie holding by the gazebo?

Fido (2006)

Don't get too attached to your zombie—or, heck, go ahead and make friends with your domesticated flesh-eater. That's the moral of the cutest little zombie movie ever made, Andrew Currie's 2006 offering *Fido*.

Set in a generic suburb somewhere in the early to mid 1950's or thereabouts, *Fido* opens with a newsreel back-story: humanity has conquered the irradiated hordes of the undead after an extended conflict called 'The Zombie Wars', and now folks live in protected towns fenced off from the carnage that rages just beyond the perimeter. (No need for prisons in these parts—just send the naughty folks outside.) Residents of a little burg called Willard live side by side with zombies, however—the undead in town have been domesticated with the aid of a collar created by a scientist named Dr. Geiger, and a giant corporation called Zomcon handles everything from security to zombie accessories.

One family's got issues, though—pity the poor Robinsons, who feel left out of the social loop. Mrs. Helen Robinson (Carrie Ann Moss, best known as Keanu Reeves' main squeeze in the *Matrix* films) wants a zombie, but Mr. Bill Robinson (Dylan Baker, the poor man's William H. Macy) doesn't think the family can afford one. He's already paying for the family's funerals in anticipation of the moment when they pass; apparently Zomcon charges a lot for head removal and Dad's decided his family will stay dead when the time comes. Additionally, Mr. Robinson's not too fond of the critters himself. See, he's tallied one zombie kill in his life . . . his dad.

Helen buys a zombie anyway, and the Robinson's only son, grade-school punching bag Timmy, bonds with the zombie fairly quickly, naming him Fido (played by an unrecognizable Billy Connolly). A collar malfunction during a confrontation between Fido and an elderly resident leads to an outbreak of uncontrolled zombie attacks in Willard—but Timmy tries to cover for poor Fido, who was only munching on the old lady who beat him with her walker 'cause that's just what zombies *do*. Fido, in fact, rapidly becomes the most sympathetic character in the film—he's just a big, lumbering kid who even learns how to control his desire to eat living innards when it comes to Helen and Timmy.

Helen finds herself becoming attached to Fido as well, but not in the same way that Mr. Theopolis down the street is attached to his zombie, Tammy. Seems Theopolis (Tim Blake Nelson) got the boot from Zomcon for having a zombie girlfriend. (Worst. Screen Kiss. Ever. That's all we'll say about that, thanks.) It's not too long, however, before the new head of Zomcon, a war hero named Mr. Bottoms, figures out who's responsible for knocking off the old lady—and spawning a whole buncha ghouls who need a bullet in the brain—and ships Fido off to . . . well, we won't spoil the big finish.

Many lessons are learned along the way: if the local bullies get zombiefied, Mom's always around to shoot 'em in the forehead, kids under 12 aren't allowed to have handguns, and owning six zombie servants means you've really made it up the Zomcon ladder. The references to Lassie are really, really, hard to miss (the kid's named Timmy, after all) and the cold-war vibe of the suburban landscapes of Willard give Fido a genuine everything's-sunny-even-if-they-nuke-us feel. Instead of 'duck and cover', the local schoolchildren sing 'In the brain and not the chest . . . head shots are the very best!' on the rifle range during their daily target practice.

Fido never digs very deeply into the darker places it could've gone (slavery, isolation, mistrust, propaganda, the uncontrolled influence of the zombie-industrial complex), but it does touch on all of these issues and more during its lovingly-shot 90 minutes. The messages propagated by those in power—you can't trust your neighbors, you can't trust the elderly, and you should never get too close to anyone since you never know when they're gonna be trying to attack you from beyond—are ultimately put to rest by the sunny finish and the infectious smile of the pregnant Helen. (Carrie Ann Moss was actually pregnant during the shoot, and the filmmakers added this as a subplot.) If anything, this Canadian film promotes a stereotype of our neighbors to the north: this is a really polite monster comedy. Perhaps that's why *Fido* flopped at the box office, its $8 million budget has yet to be recouped.

Fido Quiz

Answers on page 166.

Rating: DefCon 1

1. Naming the idyllic town Willard is an homage to the town in what classic horror film?

Rating: DefCon 2

2. What's Timmy's excuse for the blood on the zombie?

Rating: DefCon 3

3. How many of the school children raise their hands when asked how many of them have ever had to kill a zombie?

Name Game

Rating: DefCon 1

Which of the following is not an actual zombie movie? Answer on page 166.

1. *Demonium*
2. *Die You Zombie Bastards!*
3. *King Deadward II*
4. *Neon Maniacs*
5. *Nudist Colony of the Dead*
6. *Raiders of the Living Dead*
7. *Space Zombie Bingo*
8. *Zombies of Broadway*

Musical Interlude: Rob Zombie & White Zombie

While you were watching *Pee-Wee's Playhouse* as a child—or a college kid indulging in whatever was around to make *Pee-Wee's Playhouse* more interesting—did you know that somewhere in the background, moving props or filling up coffee cups, was one Mister Rob Zombie?

Robert Bartleh Cummings (Rob's real name), the son of carnival workers, was a production assistant on *Playhouse* prior to the formation of his first otherworldly project, the alt-metal fantasy band White Zombie. The band was named after the 1932 movie; Zombie has always been a fan of classic black-and-white films, even though he now directs modern full-color splatterfests. First hatched in 1985 while Zombie was a student at Parsons School of Design in NYC, the rotating lineup included Sean Yseult, Zombie's old college girlfriend. (Zombie taught Sean how to play bass.) The band toiled in obscurity until 1992, when Geffen records signed the group. "La Sexorcisto: Devil Music, Vol 1", was released with the single "Thunder Kiss '65", and immediately found a home on MTV's *Beavis and Butthead* show. As everyone knows, a positive review by Beavis and Butthead was about as important to a rock band in the '90s as a good notice in the *Times* is to a Broadway show.

White Zombie shredded its way through a few years of touring that drove the platinum success of "Sexorcisto", which led to the highly anticipated "Astro-Creep 2000" in 1995. That release produced the group's biggest hit, alternative rock format staple "More Human Than Human". The cut summed up what made White Zombie so very charming for 14-year-old boys and aging metal-heads alike: driving riffs that were easy to learn for the garage guitarist, Zombie's vocal style that wavered somewhere between a snarl and a growl, and trippy, horror-show lyrics that managed to include both the lines "I am the crawling dead" and "Love, American style—yeah . . .".

Eventually Rob Bartleh legally changed his name to Rob Zombie, and after the relationship between Zombie and Yseult dissolved, Zombie began dating Sheri Lyn Skurkis, a dancer and model who eventually became Mrs. Sheri Moon Zombie on Halloween 2002. Sheri tours with Rob, choreographing and costume designing for the now-solo Zombie.

She's appeared on album covers, in some of Zombie's films, and in the December 2005 edition of *Playboy*.

After White Zombie split up, Rob Zombie found the biggest smash of his career, the solo disc "Hellbilly Deluxe", an album that hit number 5 on the Billboard charts in 1998. The album included Zombie's two most successful singles, the uptempo "Dragula" and the grinding (but incredibly hooky) "Living Dead Girl", which charted 6 and 7 on the national rock charts respectively.

While his musical career continued with the recording of more solo work, Zombie also turned his considerable talents to filmmaking, writing and directing *House of 1000 Corpses*, *The Devil's Rejects* and the 2007 reboot of *Halloween*. Zombie's often been pretty critical of the Hollywood treadmill, but somehow still gets hired on a regular basis. Although he's known for directing some pretty violent fare, Zombie's a committed vegetarian—Rob saw a documentary in the '80s that put him off meat for good.

Despite the dreadlocks, whiteout makeup and heavy boots (he's owned one pair for 20 years) Rob's also got a gentle side. His love of classic Hollywood extends well beyond horror; a recent twitter post from Zombie reads: "Movie of the day: *Mr. Blandings Builds His Dream House* starring Cary Grant and Myrna Loy. Good stuff." Zombie's also monumentally pleasant to interviewers who are granted backstage access, offering those allowed in his green room everything from soda to salsa.

Zombie owned the record label Zombie-A-Go-Go, which produced a range of psycho-billy and horror-surf acts. He draws, too, illustrating some of the discs he's produced over the years.

And A Special Appearance By . . .

Rating: DefCon 3

Zombies aren't always the star of the show. In television land, sometimes they only shuffle into a single episode. Your job in this quiz is to match a description of a TV show episode with the name of that show. Solution on page 166.

1. Mayhem ensues when a young boy tries to bring "Snowball I" back to life.

2. A reporter accustomed to not being believed when reporting on the supernatural believes that a deceased Haitian is being used for revenge on the mob.

3. A Chef is among those turned to zombies—although authorities say it's just pinkeye.

4. A pair of agents investigate the possible zombiefication of a member of the Millennium Group.

5. In a four-part episode, our heroine goes to Scotland with her friend Zander, where a castle is overrun by zombies.

6. A week after being visited by Hollywood producer Harold Hecuba and two weeks before meeting butterfly collector Lord Beasley, a professor is turned, briefly, into a zombie via a voodoo spell.

7. A guy randomly punches strangers before the undead arise to retaliate...although it all ends with a zombie dance and an uplifting message.

A. *Kolchak: The Night Stalker*
B. *Buffy the Vampire Slayer*
C. *Saturday Night Live*
D. *Gilligan's Island*
F. *The Simpsons*
G. *The X-Files*
H. *South Park*

28 Weeks Later (2007)

Instead of picking up from the hopeful finish of *28 Days*, *28 Weeks Later* begins in the time frame of its predecessor, with the rage virus still gripping the UK in all its gory glory. A gaggle of survivors are holed up in a cottage in the still-bucolic British countryside when a little boy comes knocking—only to be pursued by the infected.

The random band of survivors is soon overrun, and in a wrenching act of cowardice, a Scot named Don leaves his lovely wife Karen behind in a room with their newly adopted kiddie to make a run for it. Karen and the child make a handy distraction for the monsters as Don ultimately escapes. Titles pitch us through the ensuing six months, and soon London is being repopulated now that the virus seems to have run its course—all of the infected having starved to death in the quarantined UK. (Again the purist howls, 'Further proof that these are not zombies!' C'mon. Be a good sport. It's the *rage virus*. It makes the undead *haul ass*.) London is a city under martial law—the US military is everywhere, and the Army is putting a cautious-but-cheery face on 're-patriation'.

Don's kids—Andy and Tammy, who'd been sent to school on the continent before the outbreak—are soon re-united with their surviving father in a 'secure zone' in London. (The only thing missing from this tableaux is a giant banner reading 'MISSION ACCOMPLISHED'.) The female Army physician responsible for clearing the returnees is perplexed that children are being brought back in—but she does her duty and grants the youngsters passage for re-entry. Don tells his kids that mummy is a goner, leaving out a few very key details regarding his yellow-bellied exit. Hankering for a photograph of their mother, the kids bust out of District 1 and into their old homestead—only to find that Mom, has, amazingly, survived.

To this point, *28 Weeks Later* seems to be panning out as a slow psychological thriller until the female Army doc realizes that Karen's been bitten by a critter and has manifested only a few symptoms of the virus—she's primarily immune, but she's a carrier. A hospital reunion with her husband in which Karen all-too-readily forgives Don for his actions under stress leads to a kiss—which infects Don immediately. The insurgency—I'm sorry—the infection is now back in business. (That's the nifty thing about the rage virus, you get all of the zombie-like-transformation without any of the pesky waiting around.)

The film abruptly shifts gears and charges ahead with all the frenetic mayhem of the original. A 'Code Red' is issued, the infected are to be shot—but snipers on rooftops quickly have trouble determining who's running for their lives and who's running after their dinner, and the order to kill 'em all is soon issued. It needs to be mentioned once more that the military forces in question here are all US-Government-Issue—the World's Policemen are back in action, watching things get progressively more and more out of control, and responding with bigger and bigger ordnance, eventually bringing in the firebombs and chemical weapons.

A Marine named Sergeant Doyle teams up with the kids—he's not down with murdering civilians—the female doctor (Scarlet) and a few stragglers, and a plan is hatched to meet up with Doyle's pal, a sympathetic chopper pilot. Scarlet, you see, realizes that if Mom's immune, one or both of the kids may also be immune. Scarlet neglects to share the implications of 'carrier', however, before her demise—which makes for an ending that stands in stark contrast to the 'happy' finale of *28 Days*.

The film is loaded with logical howlers (Hey, Volvos are safe cars—but can they really offer protection from a nerve gas attack?), and a few tired stereotypes of the US military. However, the European critique of American foreign policy here is more pointed than any BBC documentary. There are genuine creepshow thrills here as well, especially during a night-vision stagger over corpses through a tube station.

Directed by a different helmsman (Juan Carlos Fresnadillo) than the first, which was directed by Danny Boyle, *28 Weeks Later* follows the Romero tradition of the continuation of story without the continuation of character. It's a device that seems to suggest that there are a million different stories in the naked zombie city, maybe even one that'll begin *28 Months Later*.

28 Weeks Later **Quiz**

Answers on page 167.

Rating: DefCon 1

1. What is the number of the allegedly safe district?

Rating: DefCon 2

2. Five years before *28 Weeks Later*, Jeremy Renner played what real-life serial killer on film?

Rating: DefCon 3

3. Name one of the three flavors that one of our first victims gets from the wine he sips in the opening sequence.

[REC] (2007)

One can argue that the zombies in *[REC]* aren't zombies, just retreads of the infected mutants who raced through *28 Days Later*.

One can argue that there's absolutely nothing new or inventive about the kind of point-of-view camera technique that *[REC]* lifted from *The Blair Witch Project*.

One can even argue that the last minutes of the film owe everything to the climactic night-goggle sequence from *The Silence of the Lambs*.

Or one could shut up and enjoy what's arguably the best Spanish horror flick ever shot.

[REC] borrows and recycles, but the ultimate effect of this short (78 minutes—with credits) and snappy thriller is a tale that's fairly short on gristle but very long on tension. Few modern zombie classics deliver *[REC]*'s genuine ability to make you jump—even viewers like us who are truly jaded by fright-fests ought to find *[REC]* pretty satisfying.

Angela and her cameraman Pablo are taping for a Spanish TV news-documentary program. They've picked a fire-station for their next all-night assignment, and said station gets a call regarding a woman who might be trapped in her apartment. Angela and Pablo ride along to the scene, only to discover things are a bit more complicated. The cops who've already arrived are trying to deal with an elderly woman who's apparently gone off the deep end—so much so that she attacks and bites one of the policemen who's come to her aid.

Things get rapidly worse as the residents of the old urban apartment building huddle in the lobby. One of the firemen drops down the middle of the open central stairwell onto the lobby floor—that old lady again—and before long the building is being sealed off by officials who've surrounded the place. (Reportedly the actors in the lobby weren't informed that a body was to be dropped in the middle of the plunging-firefighter scene. Judging by their reactions, that sounds accurate.) Cops, firefighters and residents find themselves at odds with one another as plastic sheeting is draped over the building, but all we ever see is what Pablo's shooting—the entire movie takes place directly in front of the single TV camera's lens.

(The title is taken right from the button of a video camera. Get it?) The injured are losing blood and a second encounter with the crazy old cat lady ends with gunfire delivered by a yet-uninjured policeman.

A 'health inspector' eventually enters the building—he's wearing a gas mask and a haz-mat suit—but everyone should remain calm: the inspector's just checking everyone's blood to make sure whatever's taken hold of the old lady hasn't spread. Pablo and Angela discover that no such thing is happening—the inspector is cuffing those who've been bitten to their makeshift gurneys and injecting them with some kind of sedative. The drugs don't have the desired effect—those bitten become homicidal cannibals—and the inspector eventually has to tell the remaining residents the truth. A dog who lived with one of the families in the building was infected with a superbug, passed through saliva, that makes the infected quite zombie-like in their behavior. Residents and responders, locked in by the government, all begin to succumb, forcing Pablo and Angela to retreat to the rarely-inhabited penthouse, a mysterious place that holds the answers to the disease.

[REC] works for reasons that a great many horror filmmakers have forgotten: paranoia breeds tension, and ignorance breeds paranoia. As the SWAT teams and creepy bio-control officers outside issue instructions via bullhorn, cable and cell signals are cut off. The residents begin to show their biases: the building's Asian immigrants eat all that raw fish, maybe that's the source of the virus. One dweller preens for the camera while an old couple squabbles; all the while, the lack of information heightens the chills—we're learning what those inside the building are learning as they learn it. The camera itself helps with transitions and the ever-building fear—sometimes the camera is turned off briefly, sometimes the audio cuts out, but directors Jaume Balaguero and Paco Plaza still understand how sound can be a very scary thing in the dark.

[REC] was a hit in Europe, making back eightfold its fairly modest budget of 1.5 million Euros. The US remake cost a whopping-by-comparison $12 million to shoot but generated over $30 million in returns. 2009's *[REC] 2* went back into the very same apartment building for a second, less effective, dip in fake blood.

[REC] Quiz
Answers on page 167.

Rating: DefCon 1
1. What Spanish city provides the setting for *[REC]*?

Rating: DefCon 2
2. What was the name of the English-language, nearly shot-for-shot remake?

Rating: DefCon 3
3. What is the ominous name of the documentary program?

Solution on page 171.

Across

1. Prepare to be shot
5. *Plan 9 from Outer Space* vehicle
8. Bring back to full, as a gas tank (2 wds.)
14. Achieved or reached
16. *Aladdin* setting
17. Riddle, Part 1 (2 wds.)
18. French zombie film *La Horde* director, ___ Gens
19. Comic strip sound of fear
20. "Yadda, yadda, yadda"
21. *The Serpent and the Rainbow* star, ___ Pullman
22. Bottom-of-the-barrel bit
24. It may be easily bruised
26. They're worn under sneakers
30. Dashboard abbr. on a hearse
33. Meg Tilly horror film: ___ *Dark Night*
35. Colorado resort
36. Riddle, Part 2 (3 wds.)
41. Dove's sound
42. Bon ___ (witticism)
43. Nightmare street
44. Turkish title
45. Kitchen meas.
46. Time in history
47. Riddle, Part 3 (2 wds.)
50. Expert on zombies
52. Dead heat?
53. Pigs' digs
54. Change a zombies movie script
56. Mothra's birthing orb
58. Dutch cheese
62. Sound made by creature in *SSSSSSS* (1973)
64. Grazing spot
67. Poem of praise: "A Zombie's ___"
68. Professor's goal
71. Answer to riddle (2 wds.)
73. Come out of hiding, like a vampire at night
74. Christopher Nolan sleepy film title from 2002
75. ___ Butter cookies
76. NYC clock setting
77. Without, in France

Down

1. Handled roughly, like a werewolf
2. "A zombie by any ___ name..."
3. Anti-vampire weapon
4. What zombies do to victims' innards
5. Military group
6. Fight with epees
7. Freakish
8. "Zombie ___", video game for hacks?
9. Face-to-face exams
10. Drooling dogs trainer of note
11. Japanese zombie sash
12. Fee-___-fo-fum
13. Way off, like Transylvania
15. Old White House nickname
21. Miniature ornamental tree
23. Clock standard: Abbr.
25. Figured out
27. Prickly plants
28. Mall stand
29. Incline
31. Veep's boss
32. Spartan serf
34. Barely beats
36. Charlton Heston is *The ___ Man* (1971)
37. Internet discussion area on zombies
38. Wide-eyed gaze, after seeing a zombie
39. Show biz awards for *Zombie Hunters: City of the Dead*
40. Kiln

48. What a soon-to-be victim might do
49. Caustic substance
51. Escaped from a zombie in one piece
55. Funeral hymn
57. Hidden valleys
59. *Tangled* witch voicer, ___ Murphy
60. Supplemental software
61. Tablelands
63. Clairvoyant
65. Right on the map
66. Hubbub
68. Number of little Indians in Agatha Christie thriller title
69. Relative of an ostrich
70. Human cannonball catcher
71. Expire at the hands of a zombie
72. Mummy trio?

Aaah! Zombies!! (aka *Wasting Away*, 2007)

A quartet of friends—All-American boy and girl tentatively trying to become a couple, wiseacre knucklehead and the smart brunette he split with—realize that the world has suddenly become more than a little . . . strange. Joined by a self-described military man, they slowly realize that they're targets—everyone else has gone mad from some kind of 'infection', and every other member of the planet wants 'em dead.

Sounds like a pretty typical setup for a zombie flick, right?

It is, but with one very, very big twist: our heroes are the zombies, and the 'infected' are just regular folks trying not to be devoured.

Aaah! Zombies!! opens with a military experiment gone horribly wrong: after being injected with a virulent green goo, a private is instantly turned from living soldier into undead cannibal. A lab-coated Dr. Richter (Jack Orend—who also played Nazi #3 in *The Blues Brothers*) makes arrangements to get rid of the stuff, so barrels labeled as baby formula are loaded onto a truck—which, of course, crashes. One barrel winds up behind a bowling alley and leaks into the soft-serve ice-cream-base stored out back in the alley in a clear violation of every health code in the U.S.

Tim (Michael Grant Terry, a regular on the TV show *Bones*), a clean cut gent who works at the alley, loads up the ice cream machine for his pals: Cindy, a girl he's crushing on (Betsy Beutler, a sometime *Scrubs* hottie), knucklehead Mike (Matthew Davis, 'Warner' from *Legally Blonde*) and Mike's ex Vanessa (smoky television bit-player Julianna Robinson). Up to this point everything save the green goo appears in black and white, but after our foursome ingests the stuff, convulses, and becomes clearly zombiefied for the viewer's benefit, we're suddenly thrust into their world, which is a colorful and normal place.

The gimmick works brilliantly here; our leads see one another in a perfectly normal state in the color sequences. The B&W viewpoint of the rest of the planet shows the zombies as they appear to the living: veiny, stumbling, rotting ghouls without pupils. A military man by the name of Nick Steele (Colby French, who plays it like a lost Belushi brother) crosses paths with the four and has what he thinks is an explanation: they've accidentally ingested a serum that makes them 'super soldiers'. This explains the group's newfound physical strength and their odd new habit of shedding body parts—their genetic makeup has been altered so that they're streamlining themselves by dropping off useless tissue. Ugh.

A good bit of zombie behavior is explained from the ghoul's point of view as this comedic nightmare progresses: the living move at extremely high rates of speed and speak like Alvin and the Chipmunks. (Zombies' brain waves slow down in the second life—get it? That's why they stagger.) The realization that human flesh is now really, really tasty provides some morbidly comic moments for Mike—he constructs margaritas from grey matter and indulges in a brain taco made from the remains of a dead Mexican chef.

Eventually Nick is captured by the military, and Dr. Richter and a Colonel South (Richard Riehle, best known as Tom, the 'Jump to Conclusions Mat' inventor in Mike Judge's *Office Space*) hook Nick up to some gear that accelerates his brain waves. They're able to tell Nick what's really going on. Nick breaks free from his captors and informs the others—who set out to recruit more ghouls for a zombie paradise in California's central valley.

The million-dollar budget is used wisely here—there's not a lot of gore, the transitions from one point-of-view to another are seamless, and the acting is generally above par. The film suffers from a script that tries more for cheap laughs than either genuine chills or social commentary. Nods to racism and cult-following aren't really fleshed out in a way that carries any weight, and the film's final scene seems entirely out of place after a satisfying look at our heros' settlement 'Zombietown'. Still, there are some gags that work in this one—the sitcom love scenes between Tim and Cindy are properly cheesy, and the reduction of Mike's character to a talking head being hauled around in a bowling-ball-bag is downright inspired.

Aaah! Zombies!! (aka Wasting Away) Quiz
Answers on page 167.

Rating: DefCon 1
   1. What object is swung at our "heroes" when they enter the bar?

Rating: DefCon 2
   2. Who gets hit in the head with a bowling ball?

Rating: DefCon 3
   3. What letter in the "Bowl" sign outside the alley isn't lit?

Diary of the Dead (2007)

Yes, this 2007 offering comes from the mind of George Romero. But it's not the next in line in the narrative that began with *Night of the Living Dead*, this one is something of a reboot—a new story clearly influenced by hand-held camera films such as *The Blair Witch Project* and *Cloverfield*.

The gimmick in *Diary of the Dead* is that we are watching a film-within-a-film. "If this turns out to be a big thing, I just want to record it," says the guy behind the camera who is trying to get a group of friends home during a zombie epidemic. And he—and his companions—try to do just that, a task that isn't always easy under life and death (and undeath) circumstances. Their footage is supplemented with surveillance recordings, news clips, and other found footage adding up to a document meant to assist those of us who might have survived.

Thanks, guys.

What starts like another effort to join the *Blair Witch* bandwagon actually grows into a fairly smart, introspective and creatively gorey trek into the takeover genre (even if the scene where the Texas gal escapes from the mummified zombie goes for *Shawn of the Dead*-style laughs and, instead, stretches the credibility of *Diary*). The film was criticized for being less scary than other Romero offerings, but give it points for being less about cheap shocks and more about the mathematical futility of living in a zombified world.

Once again, Romero's use of totally unknown actors is a big plus. From the beginning, the audience has no idea who among the supporting characters is going to survive for five minutes, let along the length of the film (we at least know that the film-within-a-film narrator is going to make it to at least the film-within-a-film editing stage). And that tension pushes us toward engagement.

A shame about the farmer, though. We won't spoil his creative demise.

Diary of the Dead Quiz

Answers on page 167.

Rating: DefCon 1

1. What kind of marauding monster movie were the students making when the zombie attacks began?

Rating: DefCon 2

2. How does Samuel communicate?

Rating: DefCon 3

3. What's our first indication that the birthday party clown is a zombie?

Planet Terror (2007)

It's impossible to dislike a movie as ridiculous as *Planet Terror* when said movie is TRYING to be as ridiculous as *Planet Terror*.

Designed for release as half of a double-feature with Quentin Tarantino's *Death Proof* (a tribute to stuntwomen, classic cars, Kurt Russell and the coffee klatch), *Planet Terror* is a nod to ultra-low-budget T&A laden sexploitation horror flicks of the '70s. The film's writer and director is Robert Rodriguez, who's given the world everything from *El Mariachi* to *Sin City* to *Spy Kids*. Rodriguez also scored the film.

The undeniably gorgeous Rose McGowan plays Cherry Darling, a go-go dancer (not a stripper, mind you) who's on the outs with her boyfriend Wray, owner of the towing service Wray's Wreckage. Wray's good friends with JT, who owns a BBQ shack that he rents from his brother, the local sheriff of the Texas hamlet where the action's set. Sheriff Hague is played with tongue nicely in cheek by Michael Biehn, hero of both the first *Terminator* film and *Aliens*. Everybody, in fact, seems to be enjoying the living heck out of themselves in this outrageous splatterama—there's no other word to describe the volume, speed and trajectory of the fluid issuing from both human and zombie injuries.

Josh Brolin gets in on the act as an emergency room doctor who's a) seeing a whole lot of weird infections rolling through the doors and b) out to bust his wife for having an affair with someone—a someone that turns out to be a gal (played by Stacy Ferguson, or 'Fergie', of Black Eyed Peas and solo pop fame). *Planet Terror* is well aware of both what it's paying tribute to and what its young, mostly male hipster audience would enjoy: the implied sex includes quite a bit of lesbianism. Brolin's wife is played by Marley Shelton, who seems to be channeling every still from *Valley of the Dolls*—the woman has an uncanny ability to pose like the woman on the back of a trucker's mud flaps.

Not that McGowan can't strike the centerfold look. Even as she's reduced to staggering on one natural leg and one table leg, Cherry remains spunky, smokin' and able to bring the patter to any scene she's in, even when she's asked to trade sentence fragments with producer Tarantino playing a deranged soldier (billed in the credits as 'Rapist #1', something Quentin might've enjoyed a tad too much. Tarantino also delivers the film's biggest groaner, referring to amputee Cherry as 'Peggy'.).

El Wray (Freddy Rodriguez) eventually becomes the de facto leader of the survivors, outfitting Cherry with one of the most silly and inventive devices ever handed any heroine in a horror flick—she gets a machine gun for a prosthetic leg. The film loads everything into its roughly 90 minutes: gratuitous skin, the most pus-filled, leprous zombies ever to grace the screen, a terrible lesson regarding kids and handguns, even Bruce Willis playing a military man who's both the guy who killed Bin Laden and the catalyst for the infection. Oh, yeah, we're also party to the search for the perfect rib sauce.

Planet Terror is notable for reasons beyond its coupling as part of a Robert Rodriguez/Qunetin Tarantino *Grindhouse* double feature (that flopped at the box office, by the way).

Like *Death Proof*, *Planet Terror* is shot on what appears to be high-speed junk celluloid that's been scratched and damaged. So damaged, in fact, that the film appears to actually jam and burn during the coupling of Cherry and El Wray in JT's bedroom at the back of his barbecue joint, 'The Bone Shack'. A title card explaining 'MISSING REEL' appears and gives way to the funniest shot in the film: we return to see that 'The Bone Shack' is now completely engulfed in flames and the relationship between the Sheriff and Wray has somehow morphed from mistrust to mutual admiration as they nurse their wounds from what must have been a pretty rough zombie attack. Later, the survivors make their escape as El Wray leads them hunched on a kids' mini-bike, a knees-akimbo sight gag which diminishes his cool factor considerably. Lastly, the first signs of zombie-symptoms happen to turn up at an ER—making *Planet Terror* one of the few horror films to point out that a hospital is where any outbreak might first come to be noticed.

Planet Terror Quiz

Answers on page 167.

Rating: DefCon 1

1. What fake preview shown during *Grindhouse* actually became a feature film?

Rating: DefCon 2

2. Quentin Tarantino's character says that, while he hasn't seen a stripper with one leg, he has seen a stripper with this many toes?

Rating: DefCon 3

3. What element, usually annoying in movie theaters, has been added to the *Planet Terror* DVD as an additional track?

Dance of the Dead (2008)

A caretaker toils away in his graveyard, trying to right a vase that keeps tumbling from its spot by a headstone. A hand plunges up from below, and calmly, the caretaker lops the hand from its arm. Nonplussed, the caretaker tosses the still-animated hand into a wheelbarrow that already contains a collection of still-twitching body parts. The camera pulls to a wide shot—and we can't help but notice that the cemetery is situated right next to the three ominous cooling towers of the local power plant.

That's the setup for the re-animation of those passed in *Dance of the Dead*, a pricelessly funny low-budget flick from USC film grad Gregg Bishop. Scripted by fellow USC alum Joe Ballarini, *Dance of the Dead* follows the prom-night travails of the on-again, off-again couple Jimmy and Lindsey, the high school sci-fi club geeks, a cheerleader whose date couldn't make the big night (bad plate of spinach, apparently), the headed-for-juvie Kyle, a punk band and the prom queen and her court.

Dance of the Dead unfolds over the course of a single day and night in an American suburban town in Georgia as the kids are prepping for the big dance. Lindsey and Jimmy quarrel, and Linds decides to head to the dance with Mitch—student body president and driver of a really bitchin' Camaro. Mitch parks with Lindsey at the local graveyard—it's got a great view, really it does!—as the sci-fi club is monkeying around on the grounds with some new paranormal detection equipment. It's not long before the dead are plunging up out of the earth and running after everything with a heartbeat. Mitch is dispatched along with a member of the sci-fi club; Jimmy, cheerleader Gwen and the certifiably insane Kyle eventually meet up with the graveyard survivors by taking refuge in—a funeral home.

The kids make their escape and stumble across their military-trained, gung-ho crazy PE teacher and football coach, who outfits the guys and gals with a variety of weapons and combat footwear. The group determines that the prom is easy pickin's for the zombies—and it's time to intervene. (Lindsey, by the way, planned the big night, and she's a little miffed that things aren't working out as she'd hoped.) On the way over to the high school gym, they discover that the local punk band has been able to survive for five hours simply by playing—the undead are completely distracted by hardcore music and mull around like sheep as Coach picks 'em off with an automatic rifle. Coach is also packing a good bit of *C4*, and the balance of the film revolves around a somewhat-badly-executed plan to blow up the high school with the zombies still inside.

Dance of the Dead offers the kind of sight gags and situational antics that informed *Zombieland* and *Shaun of the Dead*, but it neatly mixes in a Ferris-Bueller like sensibility—it knows how high schoolers act, talk and prioritize. (In the midst of a zombie attack, Lindsey calls a girlfriend on her cell—the cheerleader chimes in, "Tell her I said hi!") Kyle, the bully, turns out to be a critical ally until he's bitten, and the lead sci-fi geek Jules gets to save the prom queen after her king is devoured. A bastard of a biology teacher is attacked by a re-animated frog that his students had readied for dissection, and the gym teacher buys everyone a meal after the mission's accomplished—pancakes are on coach.

Director Bishop had attempted to pitch the script on numerous occasions by wielding his cred at USC—he'd created a short called *Voodoo* that's shown to incoming film students along with George Lucas's *THX 1138* and Robert Zemeckis's *The Lift*. Unable to get the backing for *Dance*, Bishop knocked out a supernatural thriller called *The Other Side* in 2006 for a reported budget of 15K to prove he could grind out a feature. Producer Ehud Bleiberg liked Bishop's work, and after a very brief theatrical release *Dance* went to DVD, part of Ghost House Underground, a distribution partnership headed up by indy horror auteur Sam Raimi. *Dance* has also been shown at numerous film festivals, notably South by Southwest, where it received a warm reception.

Dance of the Dead Quiz

Answers on page 167.

Rating: DefCon 1

1. When our heroes are in the middle of the dance floor, she has a hatchet. What weapon does he carry?

Rating: DefCon 2

2. *Dance of the Dead* is also the title of a teen-focused post-apocalypse film made for TV's "Masters of Horror" series. It was directed by what horror movie legend (Hint: He also helmed *Poltergeist*)?

Rating: DefCon 3

3. What is used to cut off the hand in the opening sequence in the graveyard?

Deadgirl (2008)

Just when you thought nearly every aspect of the genre has pretty much been exhausted, just when you think no one, absolutely no one, could come along with something that might induce queasiness in a brand, spankin' new zombiefied way, along comes *Deadgirl*.

Yikes.

Imagine *Risky Business*—except imagine the hooker's dead. Well, kind of.

Rickie (Shiloh Fernandez, who definitely looks like a young Joaquin Phoenix) and JT (Noah Segan—think Christian Slater, kinda) are two high-schoolers one bad break away from incarceration. One warm afternoon, the pair ditches school and go beer-drinkin' and hell-raisin' in a local abandoned insane asylum. There they find, behind a door that's been rusted shut for what appears to be a very long time, a lithe young naked lass under a plastic tarp. She's tied down, she's dirty—and she appears to be alive. JT makes the suggestion that only a sick teenage delinquent could make in this instance—and Rickie, appearing fairly revolted, bolts after a moral disagreement between the friends.

The following day, JT reveals to Rickie that his newfound love interest likes to try to bite—and that she cannot be killed. JT had choked the girl in a fit of rage, then beat her, then shot her, and . . . guess what? Like the audience—still here?—Rickie remains disturbed by the notion, yet vows his too-enthusiastic pal to a code of silence, which JT immediately breaks by inviting Wheeler (Eric Podnar, frontman for the indie-rock group Falling Still, and who dresses like Jimbo Jones from *The Simpsons*), a fellow punk who indulges gleefully.

Rickie, alas, has designs on JoAnn, (redhead Candice Accola), a real flesh-and-blood gal with whom he'd shared his first kiss. His fumbling attempts at romance with the young lady leads to a beat-down from said young lady's jock-star boyfriend Johnny—and eventually Johnny discovers the zombie love-slave arrangement set up by Rickie's pals. The most unsexy sex scene ever filmed ensues. Johnny is bitten where no man should be bitten, Johnny is zombiefied, and JT and Wheeler ultimately realize that if more young ladies are gnawed on by their undead girlfriend, more undead girlfriends might just be on the horizon. The final sequence culminates in one of the most disturbing 'happy' endings any coming of age film has had the onions to put up on the big screen. As is often the case in zombie movies, we the living turn out to be quite a bit nastier than our undead brethren.

Deadgirl is revolting, disgusting, awful—and somehow as horribly compelling as any zombie film in the past decade. Some critics loathe the film for one of the central plot devices—hey, zombie gal or not, it's still rape—and they're right to point this out. (If you portray the very thing you purport to be exposing as evil, are you any better for it?) But fear not . . . misogynists get their logical comeuppance.

Except for one.

Morally bankrupt, gloomy, morbid, dank—and shot through with the kind of teen-angst-from-class-warfare tensions that made John Hughes millions—*Deadgirl* inevitably angers more than entertains most viewers. Be forewarned—if you're easily offended by lots of skin, lots of skin being eaten, or relations between teenage gents and their undead sex slaves, then you'd probably be better off watching *The Evil Dead* one more time.

One of the executive producers on this bloody Valentine is Chris Webster, whose previous credits include both *Heathers* (about those on the outside of the popular crowd at school) and *Hellraiser* (about an undead lover trying to get his mojo back). Looks like Chris found a script to produce that managed to tie in both concepts.

Deadgirl Quiz
Answers on page 167.

Rating: DefCon 1
　1. In what city does *Deadgirl* take place?

Rating: DefCon 2
　2. What do our heroes find *before* they find the naked girl?

Rating: DefCon 3
　3. In the beginning of the film, Rickie is asked for a word that starts with F but ends in Uck. The answer isn't a expletive. What is the word?

Solution on page 172.

Across

1. Afternoon socials with few zombies
5. Real estate in Romero's fourth in a series
9. South of the border zombie greeting: Buenos ___
13. Enemy leader?
14. A zombie in the basement? "I had no ___!"
15. Planet that stood still in 1951 and 2008 films
16. Outdated video format, for short
17. Whirling current
18. J.J. Abrams' "Clover," to New York City's population
19. Container for a zombie's ashes
21. After-bath powder
23. Uniform fabric
26. Chainsaw or gun, e.g., on a zombie movie set
28. Slight advantage
32. Scare word
33. Customers
36. ___ and outs
37. Cell-phone button
39. "___ alive!"
40. Appear out of nowhere in a zombie film
42. Phrase that follows 5- and 82-Across and 4-, 9-, 61- and 64-Down (3 wds.)
46. Spa feature
49. Grassland
50. "I dare you!" (2 wds.)
54. *48 ___*
55. Things held by Moses
59. By way of
60. Pay attention to
62. Shocked reaction to seeing a zombie
63. Jamie Lee Curtis thriller: *Terror ___*
65. Hollywood favorite
67. Deli bread
68. Former Portuguese colony in China

71. Stretched vehicle driven by creepster in *Burnt Offerings*
74. Stuck in the freezer at the morgue
78. Become accustomed (to)
79. Government's secret alien location: ___ 51
80. Wise guy
81. 1988 Lucas Hass film: ___ *in White*
82. Daybreak in Romero's second in a series
83. Character type with jealous computer in 1984's *Electric Dreams*

Down

1. Keyboard key
2. Bard's "before"
3. Be in a zombie movie
4. Title character in Edgar Wright's 2004 romantic zombie comedy
5. Bank claim
6. Throw in
7. *The Killer Inside Me* star, ___ Beatty
8. Ohio city where *Abe's Tomb* vampire flick was shot
9. High school event in title of Gregg Bishop's 2008 zombie flick
10. Hot blood
11. Money dispenser
12. Withdrawn
15. Aquatic shocker
20. Mythical giant bird that terrorized Sinbad
22. Suitable
23. Original network of *The Twilight Zone*
24. Unused weapon in trunk in *Zombieland*
25. Charged particle
26. Type of helmet in *Tarzan* films
27. Peddles anew
29. Quick swim
30. African antelope
31. Paranormal skill in *Carrie*
34. On, as a lamp

35. Health resort
38. Darko's first name, briefly
41. Roulette bet
43. Movie production company: ___ Monster Films
44. Smart shark thriller: ___ Blue Sea
45. Join a cannibal for dinner
46. Theater admonishment
47. "Earth Girls ___ Easy" (Julie Brown song)
48. Exploit
51. Egg cells
52. Roman numeral for second sequel
53. Beachgoer's goal
56. In times past
57. Minstrel's song
58. Hog heaven?
61. Journal in title of Romero's fifth in a series
64. Time on the throne in Len Barnhart's zombie novel
66. Scheduled to arrive
67. Horse of a certain color
68. "Cool" amount
69. Gasteyer of Mean Girls
70. Something to chew on
72. Rosemary's Baby author, ___ Levin
73. Kitten's cry
75. Stage signal to a zombie
76. Flub a line
77. Turkey, like Redneck Zombies

Zombieland (2009)

There are two great zombie comedies: the UK's Shaun of the Dead and Hollywood's Zombieland. While Shaun did inspire Zombieland, the latter's got a tremendous American style: Characters named after the towns—or dorm room numbers—that they hail from, a protagonist as geeky as Jesse Eisenberg could play him, a zombie-killer as hilariously hillbilly as Woody Harrelson's chops could muster, a pair of young female con-artists, a zombie kill with a banjo, Bill Murray—and it's a road movie to boot.

Columbus, played by Eisenberg, has a list of rules for surviving the army of the undead that's been spawned by mad cow disease. Rule #1 is 'cardio'—this is the 21st century, ya gotta be faster than the undead. Rule #2 is 'double tap'—make SURE your zombie's down, even if it means a second shot to the head. (If you watch the extras, you'll learn that Rule #2 was 'Ziploc Bags'—you've got enough problems in Zombieland, moisture shouldn't be on of them. Ziplocs were sagely replaced by bullets, priority-wise.) Rules continuously spool out as on-screen text as Columbus continues to confront his brain-hungry enemies.

Columbus—after a zombie attack by a co-ed hottie—sets off to see his folks in Ohio. He meets up with Tallahassee (Woody Harrelson), a Twinkie-lovin' redneck who really, really enjoys killin' the walking dead. The two are conned out of their earthly belongings not once, but twice by 'Wichita' (Emma Stone) and 'Little Rock' (Abigail Breslin, yes, Olive from *Little Miss Sunshine*). Eventually, the four arrive at a truce, and ultimately decide to set off for an amusement park that Little Rock has always wanted to visit. The crew stops by Bill Murray's home in Hollywood, and Murray, making perhaps the funniest cameo appearance by any actor in a zombie flick ever, reveals that, well, we wouldn't want to spoil that one for you if you haven't seen the film.

Zombieland is packed with truly funny scenes (every 'Zombie Kill of the Week' is worth the price of a ticket alone), genuine scares (notably the drop-tower amusement-ride climax) and a sentimental undercurrent, especially when we learn just who Tallahassee is really mourning (it's not his dog, Columbus). Additionally, the final scene is as heartwarming as any animated Disney picture—Columbus realizes he's got a new 'family', and the family that wastes zombies together apparently stays together.

The original script was a TV pilot, but director Rueben Fleischer helped craft the material into a a feature film.

Zombieland Quiz
Answers on page 168.

Rating: DefCon 1

1. Toward what amusement park are our heroes trekking?

Rating: DefCon 2

2. Who was supposed to be the celebrity cameo before Bill Murray got the role?

Rating: DefCon 3

3. What is the lowest number NOT given a rule in the film?

Zombies, Literally

Rating: DefCon 3

Put the following zombie books in order by their date of publication. Solution on page 168.

The Serpent and the Rainbow by Wade Davis

The Rising by Brian Keene

Night of the Living Trekkies by Kevin Anderson and Sam Stall

The Cell by Stephen King

World War Z: An Oral History of the Zombies War by Max Brooks

Pride and Prejudice and Zombies by Seth Grahame-Smith

The Stupidest Angel; A Heartwarming Tale of Christmas Terror by Christopher Moore

Book of the Dead edited by John Skipp and Craig Spector

1. _____

2. _____

3. _____

4. _____

5. _____

6. _____

7. _____

8. _____

9. _____

Zombie Logic

Rating: DefCon 1

Five friends—Arnold, Betsy, Carmen, Diego and Ephaim found themselves trapped in a barn during the zombie apocalypse. Each managed to re-kill their zombie attackers with the weapons available—a chainsaw, a band saw, a sickle, a pitchfork and a chipper shredder. Once all the heads were separated from the bodies of the undead, the question remained: Who used what weapon? Solution on page 168.

Can you figure it out logically from the clues below?

1. Arnold was going to use the pitchfork, but it had already been taken.

2. Betsy couldn't find the on switch for the chipper shredder.

3. Carmen had an obsession with Ingmar Bergman's *The Seventh Seal* and so went with the tool Death held in that classic film.

4. Ephraim lost an arm in a previous zombie attack and can't swing any long-poled object.

5. Diego was inspired by Tobe Hooper's best-known film.

6. Ephraim was frightened by the movie *Fargo* and so never went near a device used to dispose of a body in that film.

So which weapon did each friend wield?

_____

Dead Snow (2009)

Of all the zombie sub-genres out there, it's a safe bet that 'Norwegian-language Nazi Zombie films' is probably the smallest. Still, that's basically the best way to sum up *Dead Snow*.

Set in the remote mountains of Norway, this tasty offering from Tommy Wirkola offers a classic setup—young medical students tromp off to the wilderness to drink beer and boink—and wind up getting eaten by the undead.

What sets *Dead Snow* apart—besides subtitles—are a few twists that add some fresh ideas to the genre. The movie's beautiful to look at—snow capped peaks, Nordic good looks aplenty in the cast, and sweeping shots of the Arctic forest make the first half a travelogue that would make the Norwegian Tourism Bureau proud.

The first half of *Dead Snow*, in fact, is a mood-building set piece. (This is a good thing—there's no way Wirkola could've sustained the level of gore that hits the screen in the second half for a full 90 minutes without sending viewers rushing to the porcelain god.) Seven med students, soon to be joined by an eighth (she's skiing, the crazy kid) are partying hard when an older gent turns up looking for coffee. He's a right cantankerous sort, regarding his hosts with genuine disdain as he tells them of the terrible things that happened 'round these parts: the Nazi occupation, the popular rebellion against the brutal Germans, the evil that still abides beneath the snow . . .

Vegard, a member of the group who's been in the military, sets off to hunt for his girlfriend Sara—owner of the cabin and our fair skier—but, alas, the viewer has a pretty good notion that Sara was the victim who got hers just prior to the opening title. Back in the cabin, the six that remain stumble across a box of gold pilfered by the fiendish Krauts back in WWII. Wait—didn't the crazy old man mention something about stolen contraband? As day spins into night, the aforementioned old coot, camping by the fjords in his tent is visited . . . by something . . . hungry.

Soon, undead Nazis begin showing up back at base camp to filet the college kids one by one, starting immediately after a very odd sex-in-an-outhouse rendezvous. (By the by, how do fictional fat guys always wind up with hot chicks—even in Norway?) These Nazi zombies, unlike their American counterparts, are pretty darn intelligent. They've got a penchant for ripping their victims apart, and ultimately, it turns out, what they're really after is their lost treasure. Their leader, Colonel Herzog, is perhaps the craftiest zombie to ever tear out human entrails.

And entrails abound in this one. Wirkola seems to be laying out a how-to book on 101 Uses for Human Intestines, before the survivors determine to make a final stand against the Dead Reich, joined by Vegard near the finish, replete with a snowmobile-mounted zombie-killin' machine gun. The film offers some genuinely funny moments, some genuinely scary ones—the first-person view of a zombie victim watching herself being devoured is monumentally gag-inducing—and a few absolutely unforeseen twists before last-man-alive Martin makes it to the getaway car, only to realize he's accidentally pocketed a bit of Nazi plunder . . .

Dead Snow is packed with references to American pop culture and zombie films, from *The Simpsons* to *Twister* to the *Evil Dead* films. (Arriving at the remote cabin, one of the characters even asks the others to name every movie that starts with a group of young'ns arriving at a remote cabin. The same gent has his head ripped apart whilst wearing a T-shirt emblazoned with the poster for, well, check out the trivia questions at the end of this section.) The soundtrack goes up to 11 with Norwegian metal, and the special effects—including some lovely self-suturing and auto-amputation—would make Sam Raimi jealous.

Speaking of Raimi, check the camera movement when lovely Hanna finds herself trapped under an avalanche. You'll also get a fine understanding of phonetically similar Norwegian swear words are to their English counterparts.

Dead Snow Quiz
Answers on page 168.

Rating: DefCon 1
   1. Does *Dead Snow* feature slow zombies or fast zombies?

Rating: DefCon 2
   2. What zombie movie poster appears on a T-shirt in *Dead Snow*?

Rating: DefCon 3
   3. What composer's music is playing when Sara gets it?

Musical Interlude: Load Up Your Z-Pod!

So, you burned up the DVD player with all that blood and gore and undead-brain-killin'? Zombie-fy your mp3 player, friends, neighbors and corpses roaming the countryside, because you could fill an entire iPod with songs about zombies—or tunes that just simply include the word for effect. Here's some to get you started:

Zombie, The Cranberries (1994)—Dolores O'Riordan, a singer who deftly mimicked the style of her contemporary Sinead O'Connor, penned this one—which has absolutely nothing to do with zombies. It's about the 'Troubles' in Northern Ireland, and refers to everything from an early confrontation in 1916 to the deaths of two little boys who lost their lives in an IRA bombing in England. The song, which was a number one modern rock chart hit in the States, appeared on the band's album *No Need to Argue*—and was performed to great comedic (not to mention obnoxious) effect by Andrew Bernard (Ed Helms) in the NBC sitcom *The Office*.

All You Zombies, The Hooters (1981)—This one began its life as a live single, then wound up on the band's 1983 album *Amore*. Like a lot of Hooters tunes, there's lots of reverb in the mix and gravity-defying hair in the video, but, believe it or not, some radio stations rejected the tune because of its Biblical references. It carries the same title as an unrelated short story by Robert A. Heinlein.

Zombie Jamboree, Various Artists—A Calypso artist named Lord Intruder performed "Jumbie Jamboree" in Trinidad in 1953, and ignorant of copyright laws in the US, lost the tune to a gaggle of other performers. Over the years the title morphed into the more US-friendly term *zombie* and the setting where the spirits dance "back to back and belly to belly" was shifted from a Caribbean cemetery to one in New York. Harry Belafonte cut what's probably the best know version of the tune; The Kingston Trio also had a crack at it.

Dead Man's Party, Oingo Boingo (1985)—A zombie tune? Okay, maybe-kinda. Nonetheless, it's a Danny Elfman song (Elfman wrote the theme song for *The Simpsons* when he stopped penning pop oddities like "Little Girls" and "Weird Science") and it's infectious and kinda creepy, just like most Oingo Boingo tunes. It was one of two cuts on the *Dead Man's*

Party album to appear in a movie; Oingo Boingo plays it in the Rodney Dangerfield flick *Back to School*.

Zombie Zoo, Tom Petty (1989)—Never a single, this was the last track on Petty's first solo effort, *Full Moon Fever*. Typical of Petty's solid (albeit slightly stoned) pop-rock, this number also features Roy Orbison on backing vocals; Orbison was a member of the Traveling Wilburys, which also included Petty, George Harrison, Bob Dylan, and That Guy With the Afro from Electric Light Orchestra (Jeff Lynne).

Eye of the Zombie, John Fogerty (1986)—"Eye of the Zombie" was the title track from one of Fogerty's solo efforts—one which everybody hated, including critics, consumers, and Fogerty himself. He refused to play any cuts off the disc live until he resurrected "Change in the Weather" a couple of decades later, and now you can buy the original tunes in a re-mastered version.

Anything by the (early) Misfits—Glen Danzig's first band, the seminal horror-punk outfit Misfits, cut numerous zombie-related tunes (check the full-length 1982 debut album *Walk Among Us* for "Astro Zombies," "Night of the Living Dead" and "Braineaters"), but that wasn't the only genre they paid homage to—"Mommy Can I Go Out and Kill Tonight?" is a charming bedtime story. Danzig quit the band after the release of their second album *Earth A.D.*, a different lineup soldiered on for the next 20 years.

Still longing for more? Like Danish punk bands with women on stand-up bass? Try the Horrorpops "Walk like a Zombie" from their 2005 CD *Bring It On!* They Might be Giants have a pair of glancing blows at zombie music with "Exquisite Dead Guy" and "Til My Head Falls Off." Rob Zombie's now defunct Zombie-A-Go-Go label issued two surf-punk discs by The Bomboras and The Ghastly Ones, and the absolutely riotous compilation CD *Halloween Hootenanny*, which included cuts by everyone from Zombie to Southern Culture on The Skids and Reverend Horton Heat to Rocket from the Crypt.

Oh, yeah . . . and then there's *Thriller* (which we covered on page 55).

Survival of the Dead (2009)

Diary of the Dead may have signaled that George Romero was slipping as the master of all things zombie-related, and for dozens of critics, *Survival of the Dead* confirmed it. Maybe it was partly the home-run success of new and inventive takes on the genre like *Shaun of the Dead*, *28 Days Later* and *Zombieland*, but audiences rejected the film for the most part, too—*Survival*'s going to need over 3.8 million more in receipts to make back its $4 million budget.

Romero followed a military unit he'd introduced in *Diary*, gave them an armored car full of currency, and had the group head for Plum Island off the coast of Delaware. Sarge—Alan Van Sprang, becoming the first character to survive one Romero *Dead* film and make it to the next—leads the group as they respond to a web spot starring one 'Captain Courageous', inviting them and any other survivors to come on over.

The Cap is actually Patrick O'Flynn, an Irish resident of Plum who's been exiled by his rival, Seamus Muldoon. Seamus wants to keep the zombies around until a cure can be found; O'Flynn's convinced that a bullet to the head of each and every ghoul is—and will forever be—the only solution. The military band, along with a kid they've picked up, confront O'Flynn at his new hideout on Slaughter Beach, and eventually join forces to commandeer a ferry over to the island.

Seamus has been chaining up the zombies he likes and executing living newcomers when they're sent over on one of O'Flynn's rented boats. When Sarge and O'Flynn find themselves in a standoff with Muldoon, they learn that Seamus has captured one of O'Flynn's twin daughters—she's a zombie, yes, but Muldoon has noticed she's smarter than some others, so Seamus is trying to train her to eat horsemeat. The logic here? If the undead learn to feast on the family pets, or whatever's not human—they might just lose their taste for their fellow featherless bipeds.

Although $4 million is a paltry budget by modern Hollywood standards, it's a gold mine for Romero, and the film is technically terrific. Autumn on Plum Island looks quite lovely, the acting is passable, and the zombie-kills and flesh-eating scenes look as convincing as ever—with one or two hilarious exceptions. Stuffing a fire extinguisher hose into the mouth of a zombie, a fighter named Cisco makes the critter's eyeballs pop, inducing more guffaws than gasps. And another zombie goes down via flare gun (they burn from the inside out, kids!), only to become a cigarette lighter for Sarge.

Problems? Yeah, there's a bunch this go 'round. Romero can't seem to decide if he's paying homage to Westerns (check the gunfight near the end), painting some kind of metaphor for Catholic versus Protestant troubles in Ireland (we're almost certain Delaware has a pretty thin Irish immigrant population) or trying to make a statement about US troops who can't figure out who the bad guys are.

Additionally, it appears that every movie band of military-monster-fighters since James Cameron's *Aliens* must, by law, contain one hardass Hispanic woman (usually played by a non-Hispanic woman). This time, though, instead of indeterminate sexuality, this one *says* she likes girls.

Upsides? You betcha. First and foremost, the revelation that Muldoon might just be right about the whole horsemeat theory—well, that paves the way for an evolution in zombie habits that could make the next take on the concept extremely interesting. Romero has also been hinting in his last three installments that Undead Americans are smarter than we think: they can ride Western-saddle, they can drive, they can deliver the mail—well, *kind of* on the mail thing. And just like every Romero film, we learn new things to concern ourselves with regarding zombie safety. In this case, for example: even if a zombie's trying to bite *you*, don't try to bite *back*. It ain't gonna end well.

Survival of the Dead Quiz

Answers on page 168.

Rating: DefCon 1

1. True or False: While the film was in development, rumor had it that it was to be called *End of the Dead*.

Rating: DefCon 2

2. Where is the real Plum Island—the one mentioned in *Silence of the Lambs* and the home of the government's center for research on animal diseases and other creepy things—actually located?

Rating: DefCon 3

3. What color is the car driven by the zombie?

We May Have Missed

Rating: DefCon 3

Once again, we'd like to open the floor for debate: not only are some gentle readers raging that non-zombies—like those raging from the rage virus—have made our list, some are surely upset that a few decidedly true-to-the-definition flicks were missed altogether.

We know.

We could have included each and every sequel to each and every serialized zombie title. But, hey, would it really help anybody to re-hash each and every *Return of the Living Dead* or *Resident Evil* episode?

Then there's all the BLANK Zombies titles. Stick any word at all in front of 'zombie', hit search on IMDb.com, and wait for it. Beyond 1957's *Teenage Zombies*, try *Toxic Zombies* (1980, also titled Bloodeaters), *Redneck Zombies* from the legendary Troma films (1987), *Pot Zombies* (2005), *Biker Zombies* (2001), *American Zombie* (2007) and *Electric Zombies* (2006), whose plot description involving evil cell phones sounds strangely like a film described during the dinner table scene in *Forgetting Sarah Marshall*.

Want to read, at length, about each of those?

We didn't think so.

We could have written half the text about Romero alone, could've gone on and on about Lucio Fulci's forays into the genre, could've dug up—pardon the pun—every Asian take on zombie-dom, but our spouses began to grow weary of all the screaming coursing out of our family room flat-screens on a nightly basis.

And we apologize. To them, and you.

Having said all of that, there are a few more films worth a mention or two if you're still hungerin' for more . . . brains. But we're going to let you match the film title on the opposite page to its plot description found among those on pages 142-143. Consider yourself challenged. Answers on page 169.

The Titles

1. *Army of Darkness* (1992)   _____

2. *Bio-Zombie* (1998)   _____

3. *City of the Living Dead* (1980)   _____

4. *Creepshow* (1982)   _____

5. *Day of the Dead* (2008)   _____

6. *Flight of the Living Dead* (2007)   _____

7. *I Was a Teenage Zombie* (1987)   _____

8. *Night of the Comet* (1984)   _____

9. *Night of the Living Dead* (1990)   _____

10. *Shock Waves* (1977)   _____

11. *Tombs of the Blind Dead* (1971)   _____

12. *Zombie Lake* (1981)   _____

13. *Zombie Strippers* (2008)   _____

14. *Zombieland* (2008)   _____

15. *Zombies* (1964)   _____

16. *Zombies of the Stratosphere* (1952)   _____

17. *Zombiez* (2005)   _____

The Descriptions

A. In this Republic serial, 'Martians' are apparently interchangeable with 'Zombies'. The invaders are trying to knock Earth out of its orbit so Mars can have our parking spot. Notable mainly for 'Narab'—played by one Leonard Nimoy. Yep, Mr. Spock himself, in Martian getup.

B. Del Tenney, the brains behind *The Horror of Party Beach*, made this low-rent epic—which sat unreleased for six years. Distributor Jerry Gross needed a second feature to pair up with his 1970 production *I Drink Your Blood*, so he picked up this charmer and changed the title to *I Eat Your Skin*.

C. This European offering, set in Portugal, boasts the prefix *Mark of the Devil, Part 4*. Apparently Parts 1-3 didn't include undead Knights Templar terrorizing modern folks. A prologue was shot for US release that tried to tie the film into plot devices from, of all the things, *The Planet of the Apes*.

D. Perhaps the first 'zombie-Nazi' film, this one boasts both John Carradine and Peter Cushing working for virtually nothing. Shot over 35 days in a then-abandoned Florida Biltmore hotel for $400,000.

E. Lucio Fulci, Italy's Godfather of Gore, goes back for another dip in the drippings after the success of *Zombi 2*. City features Fulci's typical plot device: couple A teams up with couple B to stem the tides of the undead. Don't you hate it when somebody leaves the Gates of Hell open?

F. The French take on the weird sub-genre of Nazis-turned-zombies, worth mentioning because a) it might be one of only three films to re-animate the Third Reich, and b) director Jean Rollin went years without admitting he'd helmed this one under the pseudonym J. A. Lazer. Rollin was that embarrassed by it.

G. This George Romero/Stephen King collaboration owes everything to the EC Comics of the '50s. Two of the five chapters (bracketed by the Crypt-Keeper—is he a zombie, too?) deal with the undead: "Father's Day" (featuring Ed Harris!) and "Something to Tide You Over," in which Leslie Nielsen gets his comeuppance from the waterlogged corpses of Ted Danson and Gaylen Ross (Francine in Romero's *Dawn of the Dead*).

H. Said comet wipes out most everybody, save a pair of Valley girls in LA who battle zombies with submachine guns. Original working title: *Teenage Mutant Horror Comet Zombies*, which, for our money, has a much nicer ring to it.

I. Toxic waste creates mutant undead druggies from New Jersey. So what else is new? The soundtrack is terrific, though—The Fleshtones, Violent Femmes, Smithereens and Los Lobos all show up.

J. A remake. (We hear you: Wait, what?) Yep, a remake of what should have been a re-boot-proof film, this one is directed by George Romero crony and makeup wizard Tom Savini. The update tanked, alas, despite—or perhaps, because of—some critical plot departures from the original. Or maybe it's just impossible to catch lightning in a bottle twice.

K. Bruce Campbell and Sam Raimi are back at it in this continuation of the *Evil Dead* series. This time, Ash—who just can't get away from those durn Deadites—gets transported back to Arthurian England to battle walking cadavers. Features references to awful discount stores and *The Day the Earth Stood Still*—and a nice cameo from Raimi's '73 Olds Delta 88.

L. Also known as *Sun Faa Sau Si* (catchy, huh?) Hong Kong's version of *Dawn of the Dead* features a chemically-poisoned soft drink that triggers a zombie-confrontation in a shopping mall. With character names like 'Woody Invincible' and 'Crazy Bee', how can you go wrong?

M. Apparently a straight-to-video quickie, this mess merits inclusion since it's the only Blacksploitation zombie flick we could find. Truly, truly awful.

N. The only genre that rips off other films more than pornography has to be low-budget horror. Mad scientist + mutant corpse in a coffin + packed 747 + turbulence = airborne zombie attack. Sorry, no Samuel L. Jackson or snakes.

O. Another not-quite-a-remake of a George Romero flick, this $18 million sub-average epic starred Mena Survari (the *American Beauty* herself) and future Mariah Carey squeeze Nick Cannon.

P. Starring Robert Englund (Freddy Kruger, *A Nightmare on Elm Street*) and Jenna Jameson (Naked Girl, *Philmore Butts Taking Care of Business*). Wait, where'd you go?

Q. Nope, no Woody Harrelson here—this one's a French thriller in which a funeral director tries his hand at the theme park experience.

The Walking Dead (2010-?)

We'd be remiss if we didn't mention that the undead had finally made it to the small screen—flesh eating has, as of this writing, not only been serialized on cable, but renewed for more episodes on an outlet once famous for Marx Brothers marathons.

After launching in the '80s as American Movie Classics, the AMC cable network morphed into one of the USA's pre-eminent providers of original television programming. The channel won critical acclaim and rabid fans for shows like *Mad Men* and *Breaking Bad* before jumping into the zombie genre on Halloween 2010. The filmed version of a series of graphic novels (we used to call 'em comic books) carries the Romero torch deftly: the show's about suspense and the interaction among the survivors. (Not to mention a nod to *Night of the Living Dead* with the appearance of a zombie girl who's the creepiest kid to show up on television since the glory days of *The Twilight Zone*.)

The show's launch was marketed with a 'global zombie invasion'— 26 cities saw shuffling hordes stagger through town on the Tuesday prior to the debut date. Though most critics loved the program, not all the press was laudatory: traffic jams resulting from shooting around the city of Atlanta resulted in some negative PR, as did the unfortunate placement of a *The Walking Dead* billboard on the side of a funeral home in England.

It doesn't seem fair to offer a synopsis of a storyline that's still developing—in ways that both adhere to and vary from the original source material. But for fans of AMC's offering, we'll give you the following quiz:

The Walking Dead Quiz
Answers on page 168.

Rating: DefCon1

1. The first season of *The Walking Dead* picked up three Emmy nominations. What were the categories?

2. The undead aren't referred to as 'zombies' during season one. What are they called?

3. The show began as a series of graphic novels penned by whom?

Rating: DefCon 2

4. True or False: Zombies ate with zombies and humans ate with humans during on-set lunch breaks.

5. Portions of Atlanta's highways have been shut down for filming. Atlanta's DOT didn't want to draw spectators, so what did the tell drivers during the closure of Highway 20?

6. Series creator Frank Darabont was responsible for two screenplay adaptations from Stephen King works. Name 'em.

Rating: DefCon 3

7. The comics won what award at the 2010 Comic-Con in San Diego?

8. The actor who plays Rick Grimes is a gent named Andrew Lincoln. His wife, Gael Anderson, is the daughter of what rock star?

9. Laurie Holden, who plays Andrea, studied acting under what late sitcom star?

Solution on page 172.

Across

1. Longtime H. Stern nemesis
4. Manicurist's board
9. What horror films prey on
14. Pie ___ mode
15. Classic horror comic book name
16. Antiquated
17. Certain theater, for short
18. Former Nigerian capital
19. Who's who among all-time zombies
20. Artist Chagall
22. Schlepper
24. Miner's load
25. Whine to a zombie
27. *The Walking Dead* advertiser
30. Messy folks, like most zombies
33. Dairy farm sound
34. Make a choice
37. Tennis server's goof
39. Real-life weapon that produced Godzilla
43. Solemn promise
44. "Father of Psychoanalysis"
46. Agency employing Foster character in *Silence of the Lambs*
47. Take as one's own
50. Robin Williams' animated shape-shifter
52. Marvelous, in slang
53. Schwarzenegger vs. Satan flick: ___ *of Days*
55. Destiny or fate
57. Mastermind behind a movie monster
61. Arctic plain
65. Sewer line?
66. Chocolate substitute
69. "Don't touch that ___!"
70. Circa
73. *The Man Who Fell to Earth* (1976) star, David ___
75. Singer DiFranco
76. Freakish
77. Refuses to go on
78. Network that briefly aired *Eerie, Indiana*
79. Inscribed pillar
80. Map within a map
81. Reply to a captain

Down

1. Rural spreads
2. G-rated
3. Old Mercury
4. *Deep Shock* underwater creature
5. Musician-turned-actor in *The Rocky Horror Picture Show* (2 wds.)
6. Start of a conclusion
7. Mob scene from a zombie invasion
8. Affirmatives
9. Antagonist
10. Building addition
11. "I'm outta here!"
12. So out it's in
13. Show of contempt from a zombie
21. Walgreens rival
23. Engine speed, for short
26. Will Farrell holiday film
28. Sound of delight
29. San Francisco's ___ Hill
31. Small town, like in *Flesheater*
32. Built for speed
34. Lab eggs
35. Birthing container for alien body snatchers
36. Sequel: *The Necro Files* ___
38. Sandwich fish
40. Not at work
41. Wharton grad
42. Something to drool over?
45. Off-road two-wheeler (2 wds.)

48. Shade of green
49. Cable home of Joe Bob Brigg's *MonsterVision*
51. Cousin of an ostrich
54. Most learned dwarf
56. 2006 flick: *Dead ___ Deader*
57. Mass confusion from a zombie attack
58. Confute
59. Overact as a zombie
60. Dybbuk battler

62. *Avenger* star, ___ Rigg
63. Jogged past (2 wds.)
64. Main character in film (but not game) spelled out in the circles, starting at the top and reading clockwise
67. Horse color
68. Messenger birds for Harry Potter
71. zombies.monstrous.com, e.g.
72. Golf peg
74. Best guess: Abbr.

Near Zombies

Submitted for your approval: some flicks that aren't really zombie flicks, but darn it all, they're mighty close:

The Cabinet of Dr. Caligari (1920)—Director Robert Wiene's German-expressionist—styled tale about a murderous 'somnabulist', a sleepwalking creature who seems quite a bit closer to the practical voodoo notion of 'drugged semi-comatose bad guy'. Largely considered the first true horror film ever shot, the lead creeper Cesare is played by Conrad Veidt—who modern audiences will recognize as Major Strasser in *Casablanca*.

Invasion of the Body Snatchers (1956)—You're not dead, you're just . . . replaced by a giant vegetable copy of you without any of those annoying human emotions like love or compassion. This metaphoric take on human-turned-turnip played on the threat of creeping Communism and alien critters, and was originally cut to end with star Kevin McCarthy running in traffic, screaming at the camera 'You're next!' Studio exces lightened the mood with a more optimistic epilogue. (Remade in 1978—with a great Donald Sutherland scream at the end—and then again in 2007 as a Nicole Kidman flop.)

Plan 9 From Outer Space (1958)—Aliens bring zombies and vampires back to life in what's widely regarded as the pinnacle of creator Ed Wood's awful career. *Plan 9* has been hailed as The Worst Movie Ever Made, and it was also, sadly, Bela Lugosi's last. Lugosi, who portrayed *Dracula* in the 1931 Universal classic and the evil Legendre in 1932's *White Zombie*, passed early in the shoot, and another actor stood in for Lugosi by hiding his face behind a cape.

The Crazies (1973)—George Romero sets another one in PA. The town of Evans City is overrun by homicidal maniacs after a bio-weapons spill; the virus 'Trixie' is released, causing death or murderous insanity. Beware old ladies with knitting needles! The film was remade and set in Iowa for a 2010 release.

Rage/Rabid (1977)—Rose (Marilyn Chambers, clearly on the OTHER side of the *Green Door*) has a motorcycle accident. The experimental plastic surgery imagined by director David Cronenberg turns Rosie into a maniac who can pass on her bloodlust with a lovely little nibble.

The Children (1980)—"What happens when a busload full of kiddies from a New England grade school rolls through a cloud of radioactive gas?" I'll take 'Murderous Zombie-Like Tots' for 200, Alex!

Night of the Creeps (1986)—Space-borne, leechy-looking parasites incubate inside the fellas from a frat house, making them very zombie-like. Includes the wonderful exchange: "Good news, girls, your dates are here!" "What's the bad news?" "They're dead!"

Hellraiser (1987)—Clive Barker's S&M infused tale of a dead man being brought back to life as his earthly bod is reconstructed by human sacrifices—sacrifices carried out by the lover of the undead gent, a woman who's married to the ghoul's half brother. Our Anti-Hero is trying to escape the Cenobites, a group of demons led by a gent we've come to lovingly refer to as 'Pinhead'.

Pet Sematary (1989)—Stephen King—'Reverend' Stephen King in his cameo in this one— wrote the novel and the screenplay for this literary hit, all about a burial ground that won't keep 'em buried. Fans of King have seen far better adaptations (we recommend *Carrie*, *The Shining* and *Misery*), but fans of *The Munsters* can't help but notice 'Herman'-sans-neck-bolts (Fred Gwynne) in the role of Jud Crandall.

Weekend at Bernie's (1989)—Okay, this is a stretch, but, c'mon, the lead in the title is a dead guy. Andrew McCarthy and Jonathan Silverman star as two losers who need to convince everybody that Bernie hasn't kicked the bucket. Hilarity ensues . . . well, maybe chuckling ensues, now and then.

Pirates of the Caribbean: The Curse of the Black Pearl (2003), *Dead Man's Chest* (2006), *At World's End* (2007), *On Stranger Tides* (2011)—The wildly successful *Pirates* franchise stars Johnny Depp as Captain Jack Sparrow, whose crew are all undead—kinda? The movies are big-budget fluffy fun, Keira Knightley is great to look at, and we eventually learn that zombie pirate captains get their distinct mannerisms from the Stones' Keith Richards.

I Am Legend (2007)—The inclusion of this big-budget take on Richard Matheson's classic novel caused us much more consternation than, say, *28 Days Later*. These critters are truly problematic—zombie-like, vampire-like, living, dead, living dead?—the monsters in this picture defy categorization, and that alone should've made this film a modern classic.

It almost was—but the sunny finish seemed to betray the apocalyptic tone of the film. Like preceding cinematic takes on Matheson's brilliant book—which was, as we've said, a big inspiration for *Night of the Living Dead*—*Legend* falls into the same just-miss category as *Last Man on Earth* (with Vincent Price, 1964) and *The Omega Man* (with Charlton Heston, 1971). *Legend* star Will Smith apologized to the city of New York at the movie's premiere; the movie's location shots disrupted traffic in the Big Apple so badly that commuters shouted loud enough to wake the dead.

Day of the Dead (2008)—This reboot of Romero's original leaves out that whole pesky zombies-gotta-die-first business (but leaves the word *Dead* in the title. Okay.). Here we have a virus (thanks, *28 Days Later!*) and Ving Rhames is back as Ving Rhames; this time soliderin' in a small Colorado town overrun by hungry critters.

Pontypool (2008)—If a virus is being spread through the very language we speak, should the washed up morning-drive shock-jock on the air in the little town of Pontypool, Ontario, keep talking? This one's clever—and knows how to use sound for great effect.

Zombie This and That

Like the creature it represents, the word 'zombie' is seemingly immortal. Unlike those creatures, it can be used for a multitude of things beyond shuffling and gnawing on your frontal lobes, although the meaning remains constant—it's a handy way of describing something that has an unnatural life or just won't stay dead. It's the prefix for a number of terms used to describe drugs, drink, magic tricks, financial issues and hacker strategies. Some examples:

Zombie authors—This term describes dead writers whose books are now as accessible as anything by Stephen King. Blogger Chris Pepper coined the term to make the point that ebooks have offered the most democratic marketplace available—all authors, living or dead, can be represented in a store without the store owner having to worry about running out of shelf space. This is a classic example of something called 'long-tail' marketing; the 'tail' is comprised of the unpopular titles (when seen on a graph summarizing downloads) that, when taken as a whole, can compete with your favorite Harry Potter offering.

Zombie ball—No, it's a not a black tie affair for the undead, it's . . . magic! The zombie ball is that other trick—the one that's not the linking rings or the rabbit-in-the-hat—it's the gleaming silver orb that floats and dances above the top edge of a handkerchief held by The Amazing Guy-In-a-Glitter-Suit, sometimes ducking under and lifting the fabric while a gal in a tutu gestures lovingly at The Incredible Whatever-His-Name-Is.

Zombie bank—This nifty concept comes to us courtesy of the 1987 savings and loan debacle. Simply put, it's a bank without any money that still allows withdrawals; a financial institution that's worth zero (or less) but can pay its customers and make good on its debts through a handy stream of cash from the government. Instead of eating brains, these critters eat consumer confidence.

Zombie cell phone—A mobile version of the 'zombie computer' (see below), a zombified cell phone is part of a botnet, a network of devices that can attack computers or send out spam without the owner's knowledge. They're also handy for generating fake pageviews on websites to make them appear more appetizing to advertisers.

Zombie cocktail—The story goes that a business-type had a business-type-meeting one morning, but was completely hung over that particular AM. Into a Hollywood joint stumbled said business-type, and proprietor Donn Beach (owner of 'Don The Beachcomber' restaurants) whipped him up a fruit punch whose juicy sweetness masked its monstrous alcohol content. Said drink cured his hangover but turned said business-type into 'a zombie'.

Mix the following:
    1 oz white rum
    1 oz gold rum
    1 oz dark rum
    1 oz apricot brandy
    1 ounce pineapple juice
    1 ounce papaya juice
    Dash of grenadine

Shake over ice. Strain over ice into a tall glass. Top with a half-ounce of 151 (or 'over-proof') rum—which you can slurp up or light on fire. Garnish with the horrified shrieks of the living . . . or a piece of fruit.

Zombie computer—Has a friend ever asked why you sent that email requesting that he open a link that was supposed to take him to 'Hot Pix of Naked Chix!', but when he clicked on it his computer got the digital equivalent of an STD? And you were dumfounded, since you never SENT that email? You'd been hacked, my friend, and your PC had been turned into a 'zombie computer'. Those with nefarious aims can enslave unsuspecting hard drives to do their bidding, and oftentimes there isn't even a trail like the one outlined above.

Zombie dust—'Zombie dust' is a designer drug that mixes cocaine and triazolam. The latter is a sleep aid, the former ain't. The combined effects of the two make for a stumbling, barely-coherent user who has no idea he's acting like an extra in a Romero flick. This moniker has been applied to PCP as well.

Zombie fund—A zombie fund is an insurance fund that's closed to new clients—it's just spending its life waiting around for its last customer to die. Kind of like the Bureau of Motor Vehicles.

Zombie Games

Rating: DefCon 3

None of us (we hope) will ever know what it's like to be a zombie. But we can get a hint of what it's like by playing one of dozens of zombie games that have invaded toy and specialty game stores in recent years. Match each of the following to the descriptive line on its box. Answer on page 169.

1. "This one's a no-brainer!" _____

2. "A viral invasion on a global scale." _____

3. "A survival horror board game." _____

4. "The ever-changing zombie card game." _____

5. "A supernatural adventure board game." _____

6. "Just can't get enough." _____

7. "An apocalyptic survival game." _____

A. Zombie State: Diplomacy of the Dead" (ZOMBIE STATE GAMES)

B. Zombie Fluxx (LOONEY LABS)

C. Zombie Survival: The Board Game (TWILIGHT)

D. Zombies!!! (TWILIGHT)

E. Zombies X: Feeding the Addiction (TWILIGHT)

F. Last Night on Earth (FLYING FROG PRODUCTIONS)

G. A Touch of Evil (FLYING FROG PRODUCTIONS)

Zombies Word Search

Don't be scared . . . it's just words! Find the zombie-related words that run up, down, sideways, backwards and diagonally in the grid. Solution on page 173.

Bloodcurdling	Frighten	Necropolis
Brains	Genre	Pittsburgh
Cadaver	George Romero	Scary
Cemetery	Ghoul	Undead
Chilling	Horror	Virus
Corpse	Intestines	Walking Dead
Dawn of the Dead	Living Dead	Wes Craven
Devour	Lured	Zombie
	Monster	

```
W A S Q G H L E D W O W L R N P
C A D A V E R X C R P U U N W G
K X N A C Q O Z J Y O B V H J D
F H I M W D M R J H G Y Q H P U
P R L B X N B S G F E F C G W C
U S I L O P O R C E N Y T K G E
J M N G D F U F A C R A Z O N K
H Y I K H B W A T I E O O X I W
E M O N S T E R J H N Y M S L B
B G C T T H E I D C E S B E D Z
E N T X W E U N D E A D I A R X
A I C Z N D S O W N J H E A U O
P L B C E M E T E R Y D R A C Y
V L D R V L I V I N G D E A D R
H I Q E A K Z D O N I M F M O A
E H R U R H V U I U E S P R O C
D C B U C U L K P Q R S R V L S
I I C H S C L U H L T O B F B L
Z H K V E A B V Y Y H R I H Q P
O L K J W H W G S Y J H W U N Z
```

The Girl with the Trowel

In 1936, Alfred Hitchcock killed off a child character in the film *Sabotage*. And regretted the decision for the rest of his career.

The great director was certainly willing to put entire classrooms of kids in danger (see *The Birds*), but ultimately ol' Alfred decided he was asking too much from an audience to portray the death of a youngster.

George Romero had no such qualms.

Five years before movie audiences were introduced to young Regan MacNeil, Linda Blair's characterization of the embodiment of evil in a little girl in *The Exorcist*, Romero gave us Karen Cooper—the trowel-wielding, daddy-eating pre-pubescent ghoul in *Night of the Living Dead*. Romero not only killed off Karen, he turned her into a monster; a monster so iconic her mug eventually became the image used to promote the film. She's literally the poster child for zombie movies.

The actress who played Karen, Kyra Schon, was born—fittingly enough—the same day Sputnik was launched: October 4, 1957. It's almost as if she was destined to play a zombie reanimated by rays from space. Truth be told, she was born to play Karen Cooper: Kyra's dad in real life, Karl Hardman, was also the gent who appeared as her pop in the film. Additionally, the man who played the obnoxious Harry Cooper was a co-producer on *Night*. (The actress who portrayed her mom wasn't a relative.) When the script called upon Karen Cooper to start devouring dad, a leftover meatball sandwich, covered in Bosco, was brought in to sub for human flesh.

According to Kyra's website, ghoulnextdoor.com, she bore an uncanny resemblance to the aforementioned Hitch when she was an infant. (But, really, what baby doesn't?) Schon admitted to being a horror movie fan as a youngster, watching the monster movies presented on Pittsburgh TV by "Chilly Billy" Cardille, a gent who had his own cameo in *Night* as a reporter. The dress Kyra wore in the film was sewn by her grandmother, but Schon's mom gave the dress away when her daughter outgrew it. The bloodstained bandage that covered up Karen Cooper's zombie bite; however, was something Kyra hung on to. You can find a photo of the gauze, plus more info and zombie haiku—yep, you heard that right—at her site, too.

Today, Kyra's passions include teaching art and going to fan conventions. She never acted again.

Conventions, Comics, Shuffles and Tributes

Although it's available every minute of every day, streaming on a computer somewhere near you, George Romero's landmark *Night of the Living Dead* rolls on at midnight screenings, too—and maybe that's the best way to see the thing. And, maybe, just maybe, if you happened to attend, say, a screening in September of 2004 at the Nuart Theatre in West L.A., you might've run into Barbra: Judith O'Dea was in the audience.

There are other ways to catch up with the surviving cast and crew from *Night*—conventions abound, some representing the horror genre in general and some specific to Romero's classic. The 1993 convention that marked the 25th anniversary of *Night*'s release was recorded in a hard-to-find documentary called *Zombie Jamboree*. Nearly a dozen cast and crew members—including Kyra Schon (Karen Cooper), O'Dea and the gents who played Johnny, the sheriff and the cemetery zombie all gathered for the Famous Monsters of Filmland Convention in Indianapolis in July 2011.

There's been an on-again, off-again festival originated by Gary Streiner, sound engineer on *Night* and brother of Russell Streiner (Johnny) called the Living Dead Festival. This one's got a special kind of credibility—it's held in Evans City, Pennsylvania, the tiny town that served as the central location for shooting. The Evans City cemetery is nearby; don't be surprised if you remember it looking bigger in the film. (You know what they say: the camera adds 10 graves.)

One of the slicker events that's popped out of the plot in recent years is Seattle's ZomBcon, an October event that draws in everyone from Romero and his actors and crewmen to Rose McGowan and the writer of the comic book *Zombies vs. Cheerleaders*. (More on the comics in a moment.) In addition to the panel discussions and film screenings, attendees show up in costume, which has led to the directive from convention organizers that "(n)o functional weapons are allowed at ZomBcon. Simulated or costume weapons are allowed as part of your costume, subject to inspection and approval by security."

The brains behind ZomBcon are in a bit of a struggle for zombie supremacy; however, there's been a zombie-walk rivalry brewing between Washington state and New Jersey. The town of Fremont set the 2011 Guinness World Record for zombie lookalikes at a single event during the July 4th Red, White and Dead celebration in Fremont, Washington. A total of 4,522 zombies turned out for the charity event and accompanying shuffle—live music was also provided, proving that the undead can still boogie. The Fremont event took the world's-biggest title from a 2010 zombie walk held in Asbury Park, New Jersey that saw 4,093 ghouls stumbling down the town's seaside boardwalk and into the city. Local boy Bruce Springsteen has yet to immortalize the event with a song.

Of all the tributes, remakes, and title-borrowing flicks that the original film inspired (including the German production of *Night of the Living Dorks*), one of the more inventive ideas was 2009's messy *Night of the Living Dead Reanimated*, a project that asked artists and animators from around the globe to re-interpret the images from the film. Stop-motion figurines, hand-drawn animation, CGI work—even sock puppets make an appearance. After requesting info from creative folks online, the backers of the project whittled down the massive number of submissions to over 100 artists who agreed to do the work for free. As one would expect, allowing so many styles to co-exist in a film of 96 minutes tends to shatter narrative and upend the mood—to reiterate: sock puppets.

Zombies have also made numerous appearances in the yellowing pages of the comics. EC Comics featured numerous tales of reanimated corpses in the '50's, but those critters were usually more interested in avenging their demise rather than gnawing on brains. Besides EC, an early example can be found in the July 1953 of a title called *Menace*. Issue #5 features a story penned by the Marvel master himself, Stan Lee (then writing for Marvel forerunner Atlas Comics) entitled simply *Zombie*. This particular character was resurrected by Lee in the 70's for a two-year run called *Tales of the Zombie*. The title character, whose alter-ego was a workaholic named Simon Garth, ultimately became a force for good and really didn't possess much of the shuffling, mindless, flesh-eating behavior of the Romero type. Garth turned up in later incarnations, and the Marvel stable of superheroes have been horribly zombiefied by modern artists who gleefully drape Spider-Man and the Fantastic Four in rotting flesh.

Other mature comics are plentiful, and the renderings are as varied as the artists creating these books. Notable titles include a comic take on *Night* and a continuation of the story by *Night* writer John Russo called *Escape of the Living Dead*, *I Zombie* (with the fantastic tagline "A mind is a terrible thing to taste") and *XXXombies*, a mix of porn and gore that would have made Lucio Fulci very proud. Top honors in the field, however, should probably go to *The Walking Dead*—it's not every comic book that generates its own series on the same network that brought us *Mad Men*.

How Many of These Zombie Films Have You Seen?

THE FILM	DONE THAT	COMMENTS
White Zombie (1932)	_____	_____
I Walked with a Zombie (1942)	_____	_____
Zombies of the Stratosphere (1952	_____	_____
Teenage Zombies (1959)	_____	_____
Zombies (1964)	_____	_____
The Plague of the Zombies (1966)	_____	_____
Night of the Living Dead (1968)	_____	_____
Tombs of the Blind Dead (1971)	_____	_____
Children Shouldn't Play With Dead Things (1972)	_____	_____
Let Sleeping Corpses Lie (1974)	_____	_____
Shock Waves (1977)	_____	_____
Dawn of the Dead (1978)	_____	_____
Zombi 2/Zombie (1979)	_____	_____
City of the Living Dead (1980)	_____	_____
Dead and Buried (1981)	_____	_____
The Evil Dead (1981)	_____	_____
Zombie Lake (1981)	_____	_____
Creepshow (1982)	_____	_____
C.H.U.D. (1984)	_____	_____
Night of the Comet (1984)	_____	_____
Re-Animator (1985)	_____	_____
Day of the Dead (1985)	_____	_____
Return of the Living Dead (1985)	_____	_____
Evil Dead II (1987)	_____	_____
I Was a Teenage Zombie (1987)	_____	_____
The Serpent and the Rainbow (1988)	_____	_____
Return of the Living Dead Part II (1988)	_____	_____
Night of the Living Dead (1990)	_____	_____

THE FILM	DONE THAT	COMMENTS
Chopper Chicks in Zombietown (1991)	_____	_____
Army of Darkness (1992)	_____	_____
Dead Alive (*Braindead*) (1992)	_____	_____
Return of the Living Dead 3 (1995)	_____	_____
Cemetery Man (1994)	_____	_____
Bio-Zombie (1998)	_____	_____
28 Days Later (2002)	_____	_____
Resident Evil (2002)	_____	_____
Shaun of the Dead (2004)	_____	_____
Dawn of the Dead (2004)	_____	_____
Land of the Dead (2005)	_____	_____
Return of the Living Dead: Necropolis (2005)	_____	_____
Return of the Living Dead: Rave to the Grave (2005)	_____	_____
Zombiez (2005)	_____	_____
Fido (2006)	_____	_____
28 Weeks Later (2007)	_____	_____
[REC] (2007)	_____	_____
Aaah! Zombies!! (aka *Wasting Away*, 2007)	_____	_____
Diary of the Dead (2007)	_____	_____
Planet Terror (2007)	_____	_____
Flight of the Living Dead (2007)	_____	_____
Dance of the Dead (2008)	_____	_____
Day of the Dead (2008)	_____	_____
Deadgirl (2008)	_____	_____
Zombie Strippers (2008)	_____	_____
Zombieland (2009)	_____	_____
Dead Snow (2009)	_____	_____
Survival of the Dead (2009)	_____	_____
Night of the Living Dead: Reanimated (2009)	_____	_____

Thank You, George Romero

Rating: DefCon 2

A lot of filmmakers owe a lot to George Romero—and many of them show it by offering a thank you to the master in the credits of their films. Which of the following does not? Answer on page 169.

A. *Wasting Away*

B. *Vampira: The Movie*

C. *Dead Country*

D. *Zombieland*

E. *Ten Dead Men*

Answers

White Zombie Quiz (from page 12)

1. True.
2. True. But, according to Jamie Russell in his seminal zombie history *Book of the Dead*, the play, titled *The Magic Island*—from the same producer as the smash hit *Dracula*—didn't come close to its chiller predecessor's success. "not even the surprise ending . . . could make up for the play's dreary lack of imagination and faintly ludicrous feel."
3. Yes.
4. The carriage driver—who spells out clearly that these are the dead taken from their graves to work in the sugar mills.
5. A candle.
6. White.
7. The piano.
8. Jack Pierce.
9. Body, soul.
10. *The New York Times*.

I Walked with a Zombie Quiz (from page 17)

1. *Cat People*.
2. B.
3. Betsy says "I walked with a zombie."
4. *The Wolf Man*.
5. Along the beach.
6. It read "Any similarity to actual persons living, dead or possessed is purely coincidental."
7. *Revenge of the Zombies*.

Teenage Zombies Quiz (from page 23)

1. Teen Dracula.
2. Ivan.
3. The malt shop frequented by the teens at the beginning of the film.

The Plague of the Zombies Quiz (from page 26)

1. A Teddy bear.
2. Fox hunting.
3. *The Mummy's Shroud*.

Night of the Living Dead Quiz (from page 29)

1. Tire iron to the forehead.
2. Venus.
3. In the arm.
4. True.
5. Nothing.
6. Twice. Once in the graveyard and once near the house. She also drove her car into a tree.
7. Cumberland, Maryland.
8. State University of New York at Old Westbury, Long Island.
9. *Night of Anubis*—Romero realized the reference was too obscure.
10. Hosting *Chiller Theater*, a Saturday night monster movie showcase on Channel 11.

George Romero Filmography Fill-In (from page 30)

1. *Monkey Shines*; 2. *The Dark Half*; 3. *The Crazies*; 4. *Knightriders*; 5. *Survival of the Dead*; 6. *Martin*; 7. *Dawn of the Dead*; 8. *Day of the Dead*; 9. *Creepshow*.

Children Shouldn't Play With Dead Things Quiz (from page 35)

1. Miami.
2. Benjamin Clark.
3. *Rhinestone*.

Funny, You Don't Look Dead (from page 36)

Dead Heat, Treat Williams and Joe Piscopo; *Beverly Hills Bodysnatchers*, Vic Tayback and Frank Gorshin; *The Ghost Breakers*, Bob Hope and Paulette Goddard; *Shaun of the Dead*, Simon Pegg and Nick Frost.

Scrambled List (from page 38)

1. BASEBALL BAT; 2. MACHETE; 3. CHAINSAW; 4. SHOVEL; 5. SHOTGUN; 6. SWORD; 7. TIRE IRON.

Let Sleeping Corpses Lie Quiz (from page 41)

1. True.
2. False: It was *Don't Open the Window*.
3. *Citizen Kane*.
4. *White Zombie*.

Dawn of the Dead Quiz (from page 44)

1. Philadelphia.
2. The Pagans.
3. *Mr. Rogers' Neighborhood*.

Zombi 2/Zombie Quiz (from page 47)

1. True.
2. Barf bags.
3. A newspaper editor.

Dead and Buried Quiz (from page 51)

1. Freddy Kreuger.
2. *Flash Gordon.*
3. *Return of the Living Dead.*

The Evil Dead Quiz (from page 54)

1. Joel.
2. True.
3. Candarian demons.
4. *The Quick and the Dead.*
5. Loverboy.
6. Tennessee.

Thriller Quiz (from page 56)

1. Vincent Price.
2. *Playboy.*
3. Red and yellow.

C.H.U.D. Quiz (from page 59)

1. John Goodman.
2. *Cat People.*
3. *C.H.U.D 2—Bud the C.H.U.D.*

Name the Actor (from page 60)

1. William Katt.
2. Bruce Campbell.
3. Geoffrey Rush.
4. Fred Gwynne.
5. Milla Jovovich.
6. Bill Pullman.
7. Marcel Marceau.
8. Maxwell Caulfield.
9. Sam Waterston.
10. Adam West.

Re-Animator Quiz (from page 63)

1. H.P. Lovecraft.
2. The original R-rated version, oddly, is longer.
3. *Bride of Re-Animator* or *Beyond Re-Animator*.

Day of the Dead Quiz (from page 66)

1. Spiders climbing in and out of a skeleton.
2. "The Dead Walk."
3. *Salem's Lot* by Stephen King.

Return of the Living Dead Quiz (from page 69)

1. *Return of the Living Dead: Necropolis.*
2. California.
3. *127 Hours.*

Evil Dead II Quiz (from page 72)

1. Spider-Man.
2. 'The Chin'.
3. His 1973 Olds Delta 88.

Truth in Advertising? (from page 73)

1. I; 2. D; 3. G; 4. C; 5. E; 6. F; 7. B; 8. A; 9. H.

The Serpent and the Rainbow Quiz (from page 78)

1. Independence Day.
2. Not dead.
3. Meryl Streep.

Dead Alive (Braindead) Quiz (from page 81)

1. Skull Island.
2. A swing.
3. Sumatran rat monkey.

Cemetery Man Quiz (from page 84)

1. Meat Loaf's *Bat Out of Hell*.
2. *A Midsummer Night's Dream*, *Shrek the Third*, *The Chronicles of Narnia: The Lion, the Witch and the Wardrobe*, *Inspector Gadget*.
3. Martin Scorsese.

28 Days Later Quiz (from page 89)

1. Pepsi.
2. A drop of blood drips into his eye.
3. 60.

Resident Evil Quiz (from page 91)

1. *AVP: Alien vs. Predator.*
2. *Resident Evil: Apocalypse*, *Resident Evil: Extinction*, and *Resident Evil: Afterlife*.
3. The film's original title during production was *Resident Evil: Ground Zero*, but that moniker was quickly dropped after the 9/11 attacks in 2001.

Shaun of the Dead Quiz (from page 94)

1. Cricket Bat.
2. Z-Day.
3. Queen ("You Make Me Live").

Dawn of the Dead Quiz (from page 96)

1. False.
2. Sarah Polley.
2. Gaylen Ross.

Land of the Dead Quiz (from page 99)

1. Fireworks.
2. John Leguizamo.
3. Trombone.

Fido Quiz (from page 102)

1. *Night of the Living Dead*.
2. A nosebleed.
3. Three.

Name Game (from page 102)

3. King Deadward II.

And A Special Appearance By . . . (from page 105)

1. F; 2. A; 3. H; 4. G; 5. B; 6. D; 7. C.

28 Weeks Later Quiz (from page 108)

1. District 1.
2. Jeffrey Dahmer.
3. Vanilla, blackberries and "notes of Autumn."

[REC] Quiz (from page 111)

1. Barcelona.
2. *Quarantine*.
3. *While You're Asleep*.

Aaah! Zombies!! (aka Wasting Away) Quiz (from page 115)

1. A pool cue.
2. Tim.
3. The O.

Diary of the Dead Quiz (from page 117)

1. A mummy movie.
2. With a chalk board.
3. Blood shoots out when a guy tries to remove his rubber nose.

Planet Terror Quiz (from page 120)

1. *Machete*.
2. Twelve.
3. An audience reaction track, featuring screams and laughter.

Dance of the Dead Quiz (from page 123)

1. A baseball bat.
2. Tobe Hooper.
3. Garden shears.

Deadgirl Quiz (from page 125)

1. Los Angeles.
2. A very angry dog.
3. Firetruck.

Zombieland Quiz (from page 129)

1. Pacific Playland.
2. Before Murray joined the cast, the celebrity cameo was to be Patrick Swayze, but the dirty dancer's cancer diagnosis forced the actor to step away.
3. There is no rule stated for number 5 (FYI: Number 4 is "Seatbelts" and No. 6 is "The Skillet."

Zombies, Literally (from page 130)

The Serpent and the Rainbow, 1985; *Book of the Dead*, 1990; *The Stupidest Angel: A Heartwarming Tale of Christmas Terror*, 2004; *The Rising*, 2005; *The Cell*, 2006; *World War Z: An Oral History of the Zombies War*, 2007; *Pride and Prejudice and Zombies*, 2009; *Night of the Living Trekkies*, 2010.

Zombie Logic (from page 131)

1. Arnold revved up the **chipper shredder**.
2. Betsy used the **pitchfork**.
3. Carmen used a **sickle**.
4. Diego wielded the **chainsaw**.
5. Epraim reluctantly whipped out the **band saw**.

Dead Snow Quiz (from page 133)

1. Fast.
2. *Braindead*.
3. Grieg.

Survival of the Dead Quiz (from page 139)

1. False.
2. Off the northeast coast of Long Island.
3. Blue.

The Walking Dead Quiz (from page 145)

1. Effects, Makeup and Sound.
2. Walkers, Geeks or Test Subjects.
3. Robert Kirkman.
4. True.
5. The road was under construction—it didn't work.
6. *The Shawshank Redemption* and *The Green Mile*.
7. Eisner Award for Best Continuing Series.
8. Ian Anderson of Jethro Tull.
9. Robert Reed from *The Brady Bunch*.

We May Have Missed (from page 140)

1. K; 2. L; 3. E; 4. G; 5. O; 6. N; 7. I; 8. H; 9. J; 10. D; 11. C; 12. F; 13. P; 14. Q; 15. B; 16. A; 17. M.

Zombies Game (from page 153)

1. D; 2. A; 3. F; 4. B; 5. G; 6. E; 7. C.

Thank you, George Romero (from page 161)

D. *Zombieland*.

Acroustic (from page 10)

1. TERMITE; 2. LILO; 3. MOAN; 4. NIGHT; 5. EYETEETH; 6. SEVENTH; 7. SEXTET; 8. DODGE; 9. DESCENDED; 10. LOLLYPOPS; 11. DATABANK; 12. MAKEUP; 13. TOFU; 14. IT; 15. BILLS.

Sudokill (from page 20)

TOE	EAR	NOSE	SCALP	FOOT	BRAIN	EYE BALL	RIB	TOOTH
FOOT	RIB	EYE BALL	TOOTH	TOE	EAR	SCALP	BRAIN	NOSE
BRAIN	SCALP	TOOTH	NOSE	EYE BALL	RIB	FOOT	TOE	EAR
EYE BALL	TOE	RIB	EAR	SCALP	NOSE	BRAIN	TOOTH	FOOT
EAR	NOSE	BRAIN	EYE BALL	TOOTH	FOOT	TOE	SCALP	RIB
SCALP	TOOTH	FOOT	BRAIN	RIB	TOE	NOSE	EAR	EYE BALL
NOSE	FOOT	EAR	RIB	BRAIN	TOE	TOOTH	EYE BALL	TOE
RIB	EYE BALL	SCALP	TOE	NOSE	TOOTH	EAR	FOOT	BRAIN
TOOTH	BRAIN	TOE	FOOT	EAR	EYE BALL	RIB	NOSE	SCALP

(from page 18)

(from page 48)

(from page 74)

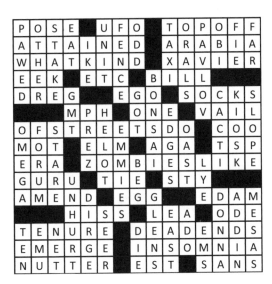

(from page 112)

(from page 126)

```
T E A S   L A N D       D I A S
A R C H   I D E A   E A R T H
B E T A   E D D Y   E N E M Y
      U R N     T A L C
C H I N O   P R O P   E D G E
B O O   C L I E N T S   I N S
S E N D   I T S     P O P U P
      O F T H E D E A D
S A U N A     L E A   D O I T
H R S   T A B L E T S   V I A
H E E D   G A S P   T R A I N
      I D O L     R Y E
M A C A U   L I M O   I C E D
I N U R E   A R E A   G U R U
L A D Y     D A W N   N E R D
```

(from page 146)

```
F C C   E M E R Y   F E A R S
A L A   E E R I E   O L D E N
R E P   L A G O S   E L I T E
M A R C   T O T E R   O R E
S N I V E L     S P O N S O R
      S L O B S   M O O
O P T   F A U L T   H B O M B
V O W     F R E U D   F B I
A D O P T   G E N I E   F A B
      E N D   K A R M A
C R E A T O R   T U N D R A
H E M   C A R O B   D I A L
A B O U T   B O W I E   A N I
O U T R E   B A L K S   N B C
S T E L E   I N S E T   A Y E
```

Zombies Word Search (from page 158)

W A S Q G H L E D W O W L R N P
C A D A V E R X C R P U U N W G
K X N A C Q O Z J Y O B V H J D
F H I M W D M R J H G Y Q H P U
P R L B X N B S G F E F C G W C
U S I L O P O R C E N Y T K G E
J M N G D F U F A C R A Z O N K
H Y I K H B W A T I E O O X I W
E M O N S T E R J H N Y M S L B
B G C T T H E I D C E S B E D Z
E N T X W E U N D E A D I A R X
A I C Z N D S O W N J H E A U O
P L B C E M E T E R Y D R A C Y
V L D R V L I V I N G D E A D R
H I Q E A K Z D O N I M F M O A
E H R U R H V U I U E S P R O C
D C B U C U L K P Q R S R V L S
I I C H S C L U H L T O B F B L
Z H K V E A B V Y Y H R I H Q P
O L K J W H W G S Y J H W U N Z

Zombie Scorecard

So, how did you do?

Well, as in zombie movies, just surviving our quizzes and puzzles is a victory.

But if you want to quantify them, add up all of your correct answers at each DefCon level—and give yourself five points for every fully correct puzzle at that level—and check your total score.

DefCon 1

0-25	What? Did you think this was a book about romantic comedies?
26-35	Barely breathing.
36-50	Glad you're on the team.
More than 50:	What are you doing at this low level? Start again at DefCon 2.

DefCon 2

0-25	Better luck at DefCon 1
26-35	We'd give you a do-over, only there are no do-overs when fighting zombies.
36-50	You . . . yeah, you . . . you're in charge of weapons.
More than 50:	Get thee to DefCon 3.

DefCon 3

0-25	Back up, quick draw. Try DefCon 2. Or maybe even DefCon 1.
26-35	Strong showing. You've got night guard duty.
36-50	Scary smart.
More than 50:	Nice to meet you, Mr. Romero.

About the Authors

Former stand-up comic and now top-rated host for 93 WIBC radio, **Ed Wenck** has written on a wide variety of topics for *Indianapolis Monthly*, *Indy Men's Magazine* and other publications. His books include *Don't Try This at Home: 50 Dangerous* and *Nerve Wracking Stunts to Avoid* and *The Hockey Dad Chronicles: An Indentured Parent's Season on the Rink*. Contact him at ed@wibc.com.

Lou Harry is the author or co-author of more than 25 books, including *The Encyclopedia of Guilty Pleasures*, *The High-Impact Infidelity Diet: A Novel* and the novelization of *Santa Claus Conquers the Martians*. He serves as Arts & Entertainment Editor for the *Indianapolis Business Journal* and has written for *Variety, TheatreWeek* and more than 50 other publications and websites. He loves speaking at SF, horror, and gaming events. Contact him at workforlou@aol.com Twitter: LouHarry.

The End . . . or is it?